Divorce?

Don't Let the Lawyers Make It Ugly.

Navigate Divorce Guide: Book 1

Divorce?

Don't Let the Lawyers Make It Ugly.

Brian H. Burke

Miramar Books
Santa Barbara, 2014

Disclaimer
The information presented in this book is presented as a service and does not constitute legal advice. Because legal advice must be personalized to the specific circumstances of each case and responsive to laws that are constantly changing, nothing provided herein should be used as a substitute for the advice of readers' licensed counsel.

The story is a work of fiction. Names, characters and events are the product of the author's imagination. Any resemblance to actual persons, living or dead, to law businesses, to family courts or locales is completely coincidental.

Editorial & consulting assistance: Alice H. Esbenshade
Technical & marketing assistance: Joshua Leach

ISBN: 978-0-9893136-1-2
Miramar Books
1114 State St., #306
Santa Barbara, Ca. 93101

Dedicated to the Creative Lawyers, Santa Barbara, 1995: Rod, Ed, Peggy, Kenneth, Woody, Michael, Peggy, Melissa, Lowell, Steve, Vivian, Barbara, and Stew.

.

Table of Contents

Appendices

Foreword

This was originally outlined as a class on ethics for family law attorneys.

The idea was to describe some common practices and analyze them to see if they violated lawyers' Rules of Professional Conduct. We started by writing several simple scripts that told stories about sleazy divorce lawyers who appear to be providing their client with aggressive or 'zealous representation.' In each case the lawyer maximized his fee, failed to identify his client's 'interests,' inflamed conflict, and stripped the client's spouse of his dignity, which was, of course, reciprocated. When the stories end, the lawyer goes on to the next case and leaves the client to deal with the negative consequences of action taken on her behalf that she never authorized or even understood.

We intended to use a panel of distinguished lawyers to explain to other lawyers how this kind of professional behavior violated one or more of the Rules of Professional Conduct.

Then we realized that none of our sleazy lawyer stories involved violations of the Rules of Professional Conduct. If we were going to use the material we could do two things:

We could offer it as instruction to lawyers, especially the young ones, on how to make money with practices that look bad but skirt the boundaries of unethical behavior. (Perhaps such a class would become an unfortunate commercial success.)

The alternative was to expand on and package the material in a way that would be useful to clients and potential clients.

Although we started with the intent of improving the practice of law by educating lawyers on how to 'be better,' we are instead providing information clients can use to insist that their legal representatives provide the kind and quality of service that's right for the client rather than profitable for the lawyer.

The chapter headings have been left in the original outline style: Each is designed to characterize an egregious misuse of the lawyer's mandate to provide "zealous" representation in family law cases.

Boxing terminology was used to describe each Tactic, but I found this language harsh, if not downright frightening. We softened the title of Chapter VI from "Whipping the Eyes with Glove Laces" to "Gloves Laces to the Face" to "Mary feels the squeeze."

I know from experience that facing the cold realities of the legal system is not particularly welcome while in the midst of divorce. Even if you still find the chapter titles unsettling, please use your imagination to put yourself in the head of the zealous – and uncaring – lawyer. This would be the sort of lawyer who might have used that class on "Ethics for Family Lawyers" in the wrong way.

Alice H. Esbenshade, MA, MFT
Editor & Consultant
March 4, 2014

Introduction

When you get the first bill from your divorce lawyer, you will wonder what is really going on behind the scenes at your divorce lawyer's office. How could anyone's time be worth hundreds of dollars an hour, and if their time is so valuable, why does it take her so long to do the various tasks the bill describes? This book provides an in-depth look at divorce lawyering – a behind-the-scenes look you won't find anywhere else. It is what lawyers should tell their clients but (for reasons that will be obvious) they usually don't.

Once the sheets have been pulled on the tricks of the trade, the attorney-client relationship changes and the change will make the professional relationship better for the client. When a client becomes aware of how he can be abused, he is no longer a potential victim for that exploitation.

Presently, six million Americans are actively involved in a divorce. We know from years of experience that shortly before or after a divorce has begun the parties establish – sometimes with a decision but usually by default – the direction their case is going to take. Once in motion that direction is difficult to change. Both parties are disinclined to reevaluate the path they have taken, and they are therefore not receptive to information that could suggest a change of direction. In psychological terms, this is the "confirmation bias." To varying degrees we all have a tendency to pay attention to information that supports a decision we've already made and to ignore information to the contrary.

Our audience includes people who are contemplating divorce and those who are in its very early stages. This is before you have decided you need a lawyer and definitely before you hire one. From those who have joined the fray to those who have become so fed up that they actively avoid contact with their attorney, the book will be useful. It will also benefit those who are fortunate to be able to make a major decision and still keep an open mind that can change course when warranted by the discovery of new facts or a better way to interpret information.

There's another readership we have discovered. It consists of people who have survived a difficult divorce and believe the healing of their psychological wounds, while incomplete, is as good as it will get. These people hate divorce and don't want to read this or any other book about it. But if they happen to get into the content of this one, they may discover an unexpected benefit. If they find their experiences were similar to the Tactics we describe, there will be an instant realization that what was done to them wasn't about them.

Imagine you are burdened by the implications of horrible things your spouse's lawyer said about you or to you many years in the past. You can't seem to let them go because of a deeply held belief that no one would say such things unless she had good reason to think they are true. Then, one day you are stopped at a traffic light; a crazy person on the sidewalk yells at you and spews the same horrible venom that came from that lawyer. You don't know the lunatic and the lunatic doesn't know you. You learn that other people can say terrible things to you that are in no way about you. The only way they can hurt is if you decide to let them. In cases where there has been a loss of personal dignity or a diminution to the sense of self, this realization seems to be enough to effect an immediate and full recovery.

Ripping off the client is not the foulest thing a divorce lawyer can do. The foulest action is interference with the transformative process by which the client's personality is changed for better or for worse. Attorney involvement with that process will not improve the outcome, so the lower the lawyer activity the better the ultimate result.

The book explains eight basic things divorce lawyers do to stir the pot. These Eight Tactics are so wicked that they are difficult to comprehend; in fact, there are few parallels from the way other professionals work that are available for comparison or analogy. It is hard to believe a professional you select, pay, and trust to look after your best interests (during a particularly difficult and vulnerable time in life) is far more interested in their own interests even (or especially) when those interests run counter to yours.

Because explanation is problematic, each Tactic is described in at least three ways. We respect the reader's time and attention and have made each chapter short. The book has been ruthlessly edited to make it as concise as possible. Information useful but not essential to the function of a particular section is incorporated into Endnotes and a corresponding Appendix.

The three styles of explanation are:

- An **ongoing story** of Joe and Mary Martin and their divorce. They are two decent people who have fallen into the web of a particularly nasty lawyer. Each of the story's eight episodes has been written to show how the corresponding Tactic works in the context of the case.

- An **abstract explanation** of what the Tactic accomplished and how it's done.

- A **detailed description** of how each Tactic is executed.

For example:

The first Tactic explains how a lawyer can write a single letter (referred to as a "Slimeball") that will turn two peaceful people into determined adversaries. A single letter? Oh yes. It could be a single paragraph or even a single sentence from this letter that will have the intended effect. Moreover, such a letter can be written without violating any of the typical Rules of Professional Conduct used by each state's Bar Association to regulate the way lawyers practice. Few people have ever received correspondence of this kind, and you have to see it to believe it.

The first chapter begins with an introduction of Joe and Mary, two high school teachers who have tried and given up on both marriage counseling and their marriage. Each is a decent person and both should get half of the marital estate, which is substantial but not complicated. (For readers who want to get a better sense of the characters, the first two Appendices contain additional biographical information.)

Following the introduction is a description of what it was like for Joe to receive the Slimeball. Then we describe in a single paragraph what the "Slimeball" is and what it does. Seeing is believing, so we reprint the letter, which consists of eighteen numbered paragraphs. Beginning with the letterhead and then after each paragraph we point out how the content has an effect that's both "insidious and invidious."

It is not necessary to read the book from beginning to end. The treatment of each Tactic is self-contained. The Chapter Endnotes provide an alternative description or explanation to what we used in the main text.

An example is the inclusion of the Martin's balance sheet as an endnote to the first chapter. The text provides a qualitative description while the balance sheet is quantitative. Some readers will prefer one to the other. The material relegated to an Appendix expands, for interested readers, one or more explanations given in the main text.

For ease of reference:
Chapter Endnote: An alternative explanation or description of a subject in the main text.

Appendix: Information that expands an explanation or description in the main text for readers who are interested in the subject.

The Chapter Endnotes and Appendices are not essential to understand the way each Tactic works, how it is executed, what it looks like when operational, and the effect it has on its victims.

Divorce?

Don't Let the Lawyers Make It Ugly.

1

TACTIC I
The Slimeball (letter) as the initiating document

Introduction to the characters & the story

Mary and Joe Martin are high school teachers. They have been married for 15 years and have no children. At the time of marriage both had just started to teach, and neither had any property. They have received no substantial gifts or inheritances during marriage. (This is how their attorneys might describe them in the first meeting's notes.)

Shortly after they married they had an opportunity to purchase a small but beautiful, well constructed, whimsical house so delightful that passing cars frequently slowed down to appreciate a longer look. For Mary, it was a dream house she had loved for as long as she could remember. The previous owners, Tom and Irene Noble, had known and liked Mary all her life and were aware of how she felt about their house. When they were both dead, their trustee contacted Mary and explained that the trust provided that she was to have an opportunity to purchase the house at 75% of its fair market value. If Mary wanted the house but required assistance with financing, the trust was to do whatever was necessary to make the acquisition possible. If necessary, the trust was to lend money to Mary with a repayment schedule that could be accommodated by her income. The trust also provided that if Mary was married she could buy the property for herself or it could be purchased by her and her husband in joint ownership.

Since they were both working and the selling price was so far below the market value, Mary and Joe were able to get bank financing and purchased the house together. Mary expected to live there for the rest of her life.

Money didn't motivate or particularly interest either of them. This was especially true for Mary. She had her job and she had her house, and she didn't want or need much else. Joe always handled their finances because Mary insisted that "handling the money and stuff" was a husband's responsibility, just as it had been in her family of origin, where her father was in charge of anything having to do with finances. Joe was smart, steady and never greedy. Under his management the marital estate was worth more than $1 Million when they decided to end the marriage.

The divorce came after six months of marriage counseling. Mary couldn't live with Joe any longer because he had grown more and more withdrawn. Joe wouldn't or couldn't change and, while he didn't want a divorce, he understood why Mary felt she had to end the marriage.

At first Joe declined to leave the house. Instead of confrontation, Mary wisely started to remodel one of the units in a four-unit apartment building they owned. She got Joe involved by saying that she wanted to make the design, furniture and fixtures "sleek and functional, and kind of like the laboratory look that's in vogue right now." As the work progressed she continually asked Joe's opinion every time a design decision had to be made. She always honored Joe's preference so when the project was finished, it was Joe's dream apartment. Mary gave him the choice of living in the house (which is where she wanted to stay) or the apartment. Whichever he selected she would live in the other. Joe was eager to move into the apartment.

In spite of the good start, the case began to sour. Joe returned to the house and used his key to enter without calling Mary in advance. When they encountered each other inside the house, Mary was enraged by the violation of her privacy. When she demanded the key, Joe refused. Their argument grew into the worst they had ever had. Joe threw a book across the room, and it made a dent where it hit the wall. A better athlete than Joe, Mary took time to find a book with a size and weight that felt right to her. While Joe's throw was not in Mary's direction, she aimed for Joe's head as he left the house; her book hit the doorframe, but Joe didn't know it because his back was turned when she threw it, and he had closed the door by the time it struck.

At the start of the next week, Mary was still peeved and decided that it was necessary to hire a lawyer to navigate the divorce. She knew nothing about divorce lawyers and assumed that one was as bad as another. By hiring George Bleedem, Mary made the most important – and worst – decision of the divorce. Much later, when trying to remember who had sent her to him, she realized that he had been recommended by no one. She had merely heard his name mentioned by another teacher who recalled that Bleedem had represented his sister in her divorce.

Bleedem filed a Petition for Dissolution and sent it to Joe with a letter (referred to in this text as a "Slimeball") that started the case off with a bang. George Bleedem's practice of divorce law was "legally ethical" because his representation was "zealous," and he aimed to "win" cases by finding ways for his client to get more than his or her half of the marital property. His most effective method was the use of sustained psychological intimidation.

Before this episode began

Joe was ashamed of his behavior at the house. He had never been violent during the marriage. He didn't attempt to excuse himself but thought he behaved as he did because he'd been very lonely, and because he still didn't want to be divorced from Mary. He had been surprised by how quickly he'd been able to understand the hopelessness of the marriage intellectually. Mary wanted him to be someone else, someone more like the way he was fifteen years ago when they met. He couldn't be that person and wouldn't want to be if he could. Furthermore, who is "that person" anyway? During their courtship he put on his best face and wasn't entirely authentic, but surely Mary did the same thing. Wasn't marriage supposed to be about learning to accept your spouse for who she was instead of who you wanted her to be? One thing he had loved about their marriage was it's physical intimacy, but Mary hadn't been interested in any of that – at least with Joe – for more than a year. Joe actually took comfort in the fact that a divorce could do nothing to make his sex life worse than it already was.

Joe suspected that people marry their idea of who they want their spouse to be rather than the real person. As he thought about the divorce he became more and more convinced that the problem had been framed as "Joe won't change." That was wrong. The problem was that Mary couldn't accept Joe as he was rather than the man she wished he would be.

He never got angry when they were doing their marriage counseling, but shortly after they separated, he got very angry. More angry than he had ever been in his life. Mary was the natural target, but he knew he wasn't angry because she wanted to dump him. He knew that he wasn't angry with himself for getting dumped. Pure anger swelled up and turned into rage; but Joe decided that it wasn't anger toward Mary or towards himself – it just was. He wasn't an angry person, so even though it felt like he was going to be angry for the rest of his life, he knew that couldn't possibly be true.

He was in this raw mood when he went to the house to get some "personal stuff" out of his workroom. He encountered Mary and was astonished by her overreaction.

It was Mary who was overcome by rage when she found Joe in the house. It was her place to be alone and to heal. He had his own place. Did he think he could intrude whenever he felt like it? Did he think that she'd intrude on him? She didn't even have a key and would never use it if she did.

When she demanded his key, he couldn't say yes because his copy was the only one that worked on all the doors, including the one to his shop. If he had been able to collect what he came for, which had nothing to do with Mary or the divorce, he would have given her the key, but she ordered him out of the house before he could explain or reason with her. He was more angry than she had ever seen him and she became just as angry at him.

Throwing the book was incredibly stupid, though it did feel good for a split second. There was nothing special about the book, the damage to the wall was minor, and it wouldn't be possible for Mary to think he was throwing it at her because it was thrown in a direction away from where she was standing (and yelling at him).

He was inclined to make contact to apologize, but he didn't know this side of Mary well enough to predict how long she would stay angry. He decided to wait for inspiration. It occurred to him that she was going to be anxious until she had all the keys to the house, but he was not going to give her access to his shop until he had a chance to remove the personal and embarrassing things he had left there.

On the other hand, Mary felt much better when she turned the problem over to a professional. She didn't particularly like George Bleedem, but she had learned that, when it came to professionals, it was better to get someone who could do the job well rather than to choose someone you thought you would like.

How Tactic I is done and what it does

Unless it came from a divorce lawyer, it is unlikely the reader has ever received a letter like the one we refer to as the Slimeball. The particular qualities of the Slimeball are that it causes the reader to feel ill when she reads it, but every line – when read separately – is arguably appropriate. The Slimeball we use is nineteen paragraphs long. Two paragraphs are transitional and the rest are toxic. They are both invidious and insidious. Invidious means they are "offensive or odious," and insidious means they are "sinister, subtle, or menacing."

Slimeballs are created by modifying generations of Templates floating around in every family law office in the country.

When the spouse who becomes the Respondent in the divorce receives the "initiating documents" (Summons and Petition), he will typically retain a lawyer and turn the case over to her. Once a person has a lawyer, he can no longer be contacted directly by the other lawyer. So the letter that goes with the Summons and Petition is the only chance for the Petitioner's lawyer to address the Respondent directly.

The Slimeball is used to make contact in a way that is disorienting, threatening, insulting, and intimidating. It poisons the case dynamics from beginning to end. The Slimeball included in these materials should give the reader a vicarious experience of what it is like to receive one.

The Saga of the Martin marriage continues

It came late on a Saturday morning by Certified Mail – Return Receipt Requested. It came in a 12 x 13 inch brown envelope with six sheets of paper in it. The return address printed on the envelope identified a downtown office building, a floor number, and the initials "GPB." It was stamped "PERSONAL" several times on both the front and back.

Joe carried the envelope to what served as his kitchen, dining room, and worktable, and put it down in front of his chair. From a drawer he took out the knife he used to open letters, a blue pen, his red pen, a highlighter, and a ruler. With the knife, he neatly slit the envelope open, laid out the contents, and sat down to study them.

There were three court forms. The Summons addressed him as the Respondent. Mary was the Petitioner. It had printing on both sides. The Petition was also a two-sided form. At first glance it seemed to have been designed to be as non-threatening as possible. Nowhere did it say "Mary versus Joe." The case was called "In the Matter of Mary and Joseph Martin, a Petition for Dissolution of Marriage." The reason, "irreconcilable differences," was printed on the back of the form where there were two boxes to choose from. The other was "incurable insanity," which Mary didn't select. He was grateful for that; he had no quarrel with irreconcilable differences.

The third form was just an acknowledgement saying he had received the first two. He had them on his table, so he signed it, put it into the enclosed, stamped envelope, and walked it down to the corner mailbox.

When he got back to the apartment, he took a beer out of the refrigerator – his first of the day – and read the letter from the lawyer. These six sheets of paper with typewritten words on them cannot be fairly described. They have to be read to get an idea of Joe's experience.

The conventional narrative style ends here. The rest of this episode is told through the Slimeball and the commentary created to explain it.

Bleedem & Bleedem
Attorneys at Law
Practice Limited to Matrimonial Litigation
123 Courthouse Plaza
Orlando, Mind 11111
888-233-3333

Mr. Joseph R. Martin
123 East Street
Orlando, Mind 11115

Dear Mr. Martin:

1. This firm has been engaged to represent your
wife, Mary, in an action by which the Superior Court
of the State of Mind, County of Choice, is being
petitioned to dissolve her marriage to you on grounds
set forth in Civil Code § 9999. We have reviewed the
available information carefully and believe that no
court would question the adequacy of the evidence
that can be marshaled in support of the relief
requested.

2. You will receive this letter, the Petition for
Dissolution, the Court's Summons, an Acknowledgment,
and my self-addressed return envelope. I take the
liberty of suggesting that you sign the Acknowledgment, which simply serves as necessary proof that you
actually received the Petition and Summons. Perhaps
you wish you had not received either of these
documents, but you have received them. If, for
reasons I can't imagine, you decline to sign the
acknowledgment and return it to me within the next
seven calendar days, I will send copies of the same
documents to the Civil Division of the Sheriff's
Office with a letter saying that you have not taken
the opportunity to sign and return a voluntary
Acknowledgment, which I take to be the first sign of
a determination to frustrate the forward movement of
the case. I will then instruct the Sheriff to spare
no expense to have you served day or night at any
place you can be found, public or private. With
concern for the safety of law enforcement officers
forced to serve documents in domestic disputes, I
feel I must advise the Sheriff's Office that I don't
know if you own a gun.

Bleedem's Letterhead: Who is he?

This letterhead is intended to evoke power. Endnote 1 tells more about Bleedem and therefore about the accuracy of this impression.

In his letterhead, the "firm" name includes his father who has been dead for many years. A single name means the lawyer is a sole practitioner. The addition of the second name creates the inference that there are at least two lawyers and possibly two hundred. The line "Practice Limited to Matrimonial Litigation" is fatuous. There is no such recognized specialty and its use is for the sole purpose of intimidation.

Commentary on Paragraph 1:

The "review of available information" would have taken two minutes. If Mary wants a divorce she gets it, evidence of that simple fact is all that's needed, of course no court would question its adequacy. The content is literally true but it has been written in a way suggesting legal complexity when there is none.

Note also how it says that Mary petitions "to dissolve her marriage to you on the grounds …" and then "no court would question the adequacy of the evidence that can be marshaled…" Without saying it, this sounds like the evidence is being marshaled against Joe. It's nonsense.

Commentary on Paragraph 2:

Bleedem starts by saying that "Perhaps you wish you had not received either of these documents, but you have." This insulting statement implies the ability to read Joe's mind, and the fact that it's correct makes it more insulting and threatening.

Joe has an option to either sign the acknowledgment or to wait for formal service. The "spare no expense" and "served day or night at any place you can be found…" is hogwash. The sheriff's office isn't into this kind of drama. Joe would probably be contacted by phone and an appointment made for him to receive the documents. Whether Bleedem wants to find "determination to frustrate the forward motion of the case" is up to him, but with a letter like this, Bleedem is going to find things wrong with everything Joe does, no matter what it is, at every opportunity.

The last sentence is especially pernicious. It is literally true, but the fact that Bleedem would say, "I don't know if he has a gun," suggests that Bleedem has reason to believe that he does. When Joe reads this he'll think that it's within Bleedem's power to have service accomplished by a SWAT.

3. Because of the facts in your case, and my responsibilities to your wife and her family, it is incumbent on me to establish the Court's *personal* jurisdiction over you, so Orders made can be enforced with the Court's power of Contempt. It is also my responsibility to activate the Automatic Temporary Restraining Orders as quickly as possible. Now that you have been served, you are *specifically prohibited* from taking any of the actions described in the list on the reverse side of the Summons.

4. Given the seriousness of the matters described above, it may be superfluous for me to emphatically urge you to interview, select and engage your own matrimonial attorney as soon as possible.

5. You will be required to pay a retainer and, so far as we know, the only assets available to you are joint, meaning you and Mary each have a 50% "undivided interest" in every dollar or penny. You may take this letter as Mary's consent to use as much joint property as you need to retain competent counsel **on the condition** that you simultaneously pay the same amount to this Firm.

6. On receipt, we will post the money to a trust account maintained in Mary's name for payment of our fees as they become due. Understand that Mary's consent to your use of joint property is conditioned upon a payment in the same amount to Bleedem & Bleedem. Unless the second payment is made, Mary insists that you not use joint funds to retain a lawyer unless you obtain an Order of Court to the contrary.

7. For your information, and in the spirit of full disclosure, Mary has paid our initial retainer. But her legal expenses are likely to be considerably greater than yours because we will have the "laboring oar" in evaluating the various possible claims she might have against you for failure to manage the joint estate in accord with the fiduciary duty you owe to her under state law.

Commentary on Paragraph 3:

All of this is literally true and absolutely routine. There is no reason to believe – before the case has begun – that there will ever be a personal order against Joe, but this sounds like he's one step away from jail. "Automatic temporary restraining orders" simply tell both parties not to do things that reasonable people wouldn't think of doing, such as cancelling or changing beneficiaries on existing insurance policies without the permission of the other spouse or permission from the court.

Commentary on Paragraph 4:

Compared to all other divorces this one is not serious; it's typical and routine. The plea to obtain counsel sounds non-adversarial, but it's also condescending. The addition of another attorney will permit Bleedem to be more adversarial and the case therefore more profitable. It would be a move involving some risks but the one thing Joe could do to throw Bleedem off-balance would be to insist on self-representation; this would throw Bleedem's bullying into sharp relief. Having an attorney would appear to shield Joe against Bleedem's tactics, but Joe will still be vulnerable, because divorce is an intensely personal experience

Commentary on Paragraph 5:

The paragraph conveys a generous and practical intent at first. It tells Joe that he can use as much marital property as he needs to retain a lawyer. All Bleedem asks is that his "Firm" be paid an equal amount. It is not until ¶ 7 that Bleedem wants what Joe pays his lawyer plus what Mary has already paid him.

Commentary on Paragraph 6:

Here Bleedem says that if Joe doesn't do things exactly as Bleedem has specified he'll have to go to court to get the money to get a lawyer. If Joe can still think, he'll wonder how he is going to go to court without a lawyer – but he needs the money to get the lawyer to go to court to get the money. In the end this is not a problem because Joe has stopped thinking. He'll do what Mary's lawyer tells him to do because the apparent consequences of doing something else are too awful for Joe to contemplate.

Commentary on Paragraph 7:

Bam! This ¶ 7 flips the meaning of ¶ 5 and ¶ 6 from reasonable to coercive and threatening and accusing. He says that his firm will need the extra money to prove that Joe failed to meet his fiduciary duty to Mary. What's that supposed to mean? Whatever it means can't be good. The content here is reinforced by the tone of the first paragraph that hinted that Joe was going to be on trial for something.

8. Furthermore, this conditional agreement to allow you to use joint funds to pay or retain an attorney is further conditioned on your understanding and implicit agreement that Mary does not give up any right she has to seek an Order requiring you to pay all or part of her attorneys' fees from your share of the joint estate on the grounds set forth in Civil Code §§ 1068 *et seq.*

9. It is our client's desire that the dissolution of her marriage to you, the division of the marital estate, and the establishment of child and spousal support be done in a businesslike, if not amicable, way, and this firm will respect and honor her wishes.

10. It is our understanding that during the course of your seventeen-year marriage, you were the primary provider for the family and you managed the joint estate. We further understand that during these seventeen years there were numerous transactions involving the purchase and sale of stocks and bonds and two transactions involving the purchase of income real estate.

11. We assume you are aware of the fiduciary duty one party to a marriage owes the other in dealing with their property. This fiduciary duty has been described as a "confidential relationship imposing a duty of the highest good faith and fair dealing upon each spouse in his or her dealings with the other." If this duty has been violated, ignorance of its requirements is not a defense to its violation and claims of ignorance can serve as evidence of such violations.

12. With respect to the investments you have made during the marriage, you should understand that while we assume for now that they were all done with the level of care required by statute, we have examined none of the documentation for those transactions and which, in the ordinary course of good business practice, would have been organized and preserved for future accounting. (I did not do this part of the intake history myself, but we have an excellent team assigned to the case, and I am able to rely on all of their investigatory reports.)

Commentary on Paragraph 8:

Oh, great. Twist the reasonable meaning of ¶ 5 and ¶6 even more. Bleedem implies that Mary and Joe should have the same amount of money to hire lawyers. Then Joe learns this really means that Bleedem gets paid twice. Now Joe learns that Bleedem is not only going to get paid twice, but he's also going to make Joe pay for both halves.

Commentary on Paragraph 9:

Why only "businesslike?" Why would Bleedem not honor Mary's wishes? Why does he say "this firm" (of one lawyer) will honor Mary's wishes to be amicable? Then there is a rather brilliant display of malevolence. Bleedem's writing so far suggests a deep understanding of the case. Then he refers to "child support." Why doesn't he know there are no children? Is he a big fraud? Is this some sort of a typographical error? If so, it has nothing to do with this case so how could it get into the letter? This twist is one that could rankle Joe for the rest of the case when it is utterly without substance. Did Bleedem intentionally include the word, "child?" If he did, Joe will never know because Bleedem will dismiss it as "just a typo."

Lawyers have an ethical obligation to inform their clients of the terms of any settlement offer made by the other side, but there is no ethical obligation to provide the client with all correspondence relating to her case. Bleedem has no intention of giving Mary a copy of this letter. Joe could send her a copy and she might be appalled that her lawyer has sent such a thing. But it's content is true so she is more likely to assume that this is what her lawyer has to do to "protect her." Joe probably thinks Mary already has a copy, and since none of this sounds like her, he doesn't know who he's dealing with. Has she changed so much so quickly? Was it because he threw a book at the wall?

Commentary on Paragraph 10:

Here's another mind-bending paragraph that contains details that are accurate and one detail that Bleedem knows is false. Joe and Mary have been high school teachers for the same amount of time. They each have the ability to be financially independent and Joe is definitely not the "primary provider." Were there "numerous" stock trades? Just a few each year, which when multiplied by 17 could seem like a lot, but Joe's involvement in the stock market was occasional at most.

Commentary on Paragraph 11:

Here it is again. It isn't said directly but the implication is that Joe has violated his fiduciary duty, which sounds like a bank stealing money from its depositors, which is supposed to be a very bad thing. Joe wasn't aware of such a duty so Bleedem has once again read his mind and told him that what he knew or didn't know makes no difference.

Commentary on Paragraph 12:

Does this mean he has to come up with records of all of his trades for the last seventeen years? He doesn't have much, which Bleedem anticipates when he says, in effect, that the absence of good, organized accounting and historical records is evidence of bad business practice. (It sounds connected to a violation of fiduciary duty.)

13. The future is now and so that it will come as no surprise, we inform you with this letter that we will be making a formal demand for a list of each and every investment you made during the course of the marriage and the documentation for each.

14. When you retain counsel, we are confident you will be warned that the same fiduciary duty owed to Mary while the marriage was intact is also owed to her during the period between the date of separation and the Entry of Judgment. Formal notices are being prepared, but you are, by this letter, put on notice that we will demand that you provide this firm with a comprehensive set of disclosure documents listing all assets and liabilities regardless of whether you consider them to be separate property or joint property, and the disclosure of all income received or earned by you during the last ten calendar years.

15. Because of the continuing fiduciary duty, Mary is entitled to be informed, in detail, of any changes affecting the nature or value of all marital property. In the event of such changes, the reports prepared for Mary are to be delivered to her in care of this office. In addition to detailed information concerning changes in the community estate, Mary is also entitled to a window into the day-to-day management of the estate, which will require occasional briefings or updates after the preliminary disclosure has been completed. We will insist that such updates be made on a monthly basis. Whether they are in writing or in person is a matter of indifference to us. In the absence of a different proposal, we demand a monthly meeting to review your books and records and to receive from you a candid report on the condition of the estate.

16. As you will see from a review of the Restraining Orders, Mary has not, at this time, sought an order prohibiting you from contacting her or requiring you to remain a certain distance from her person. She is confident that such an order will not be necessary. We do not know you Mr. Martin, but we have had

Commentary on Paragraph 13:

The axe is going to fall. Joe has never cheated Mary – or anyone else – out of a dime. He has done very well with their investments. The real estate acquisition has done very well. He's had several losing stock trades but, thanks to Apple, he has done better than the market, which is about the best any investor does over a period of seventeen years. Yet, it looks like he's going to be branded as some kind of a crook because of some rules he's never heard of.

Commentary on Paragraph 14:

The statement about a future fiduciary duty is made in a way that implies there has been a violation in the past. If formal demands for documents are being prepared (and they probably are) there is no need to mention that fact in this letter. It's included to further intimidate Joe by making sure that he knows that Bleedem is after him.

Commentary on Paragraph 15:

This is the same style used in the first four paragraphs. The factual statements are true but the conclusions would fit for a big estate with a lot of complicated assets. Here, there is a stock account and a small apartment house. Joe wouldn't touch those stocks with a stick so nothing will change there. The apartment house involves rent and routine expenses. They will be almost exactly the same from month to month, and the check register and cancelled checks will be equivalent to 100% of all relevant information. So why a monthly meeting? It suggests that Bleedem thinks Joe might cheat Mary while the divorce is going on. Bleedem has no belief one way or another. But he's telling Joe there are reasons for suspecting him of being a thief (not true) and that Bleedem will threaten him as though he were a thief.

experience with thousands of divorcing spouses, and
we know they can be unpredictable, so we have no
opinion and make no prediction about whether we will
or will not seek a restraining order against you at
some time in the future. For now, you can honor
Mary's trust by personally delivering or by mailing
to this office your set of keys to the family home.

17. You should both be afforded a sense of privacy
and safety during this difficult period. We assure
you that Mary does not have and will not seek a set
of keys to the apartment which you have just taken.
By the same token, we demand that you hand-deliver *to
this office* your keys to the family home. If we have
not received the keys within 48 hours, your failure
to honor this request will be evidence of need for a
Restraining Order, and we will actively consider the
option of seeking one from the Court. Whether we
obtain a Court Order or not, we will instruct Mary to
have all locks changed. We will also have a security
expert, with whom we work regularly, examine the
property and recommend the proper system. Mary will
be advised to have all the recommended devices
installed on an emergency basis. At the appropriate
time, we will seek to have you held entirely
responsible for this expense.

18. I look forward to meeting you and the attorney
you engage for the first of the many meetings usually
held in a case like this.

Sincerely,

George P. Bleedem

George P. Bleedem, Principal
Bleedem & Bleedem & Associates
Attorneys at Law

Commentary on Paragraph 16:

No, Mary has not requested a restraining order against Joe. She knew she didn't need protection from him. Here, by reference to cases Joe knew nothing about, Bleedem justifies his demand for the keys to the house. All Mary had to do was to ask Joe for the keys and he'd give them to her so long as he could have a few minutes to get some personal stuff out of his shop.

Commentary on Paragraph 17:

Another example of a false accusation – combined with a demand – backed up by a threat to accomplish a result – made unnecessarily odious. It's where Mary lives and it's Mary's security but the demand is for the immediate delivery of the keys not to Mary but to Bleedem. If the keys haven't been delivered, Bleedem will "instruct" Mary to change the locks. She can do that if she wants to; she doesn't need an instruction from Bleedem, but it looks like that's what she's going to get. What other kinds of "instructions" is he going to give her, and will she always do what Bleedem tells her to do? Has she no say?

A refusal to turn over keys is evidence of the need for a restraining order. Evidence – maybe, but it means nothing absent a reason to believe that Mary's personal security requires a restraining order. The "security expert" is yet another instruction from Bleedem to Mary. Can't she decide for herself if she needs more security? Here, the threat is similar to the one made in ¶ 9: if you don't do this our way, you are going to pay.

Commentary on Paragraph 18:

"I look forward to meeting you…" Joe knows this is true because Bleedem will want to see what his victim looks like. The idea of the "first of many meetings" is the kind of statement that could cause nightmares.

ENDNOTE #1 – The Martins' Financial Statement

Joe and Mary's finances are simple and straightforward. Whether an estate is worth $880,000, $88,000, or $8,800,000, the principles are described in this book in essentially the same way but on a larger or smaller scale.

Unless you need the numbers to understand the Martin's financial situation, it's not necessary to understand this balance sheet.

I. Assets

1. Real Estate

a. House	Fair Market Value (FMV)	$425,000
	Mortgage	[$45,000]
	Equity	$380,000

b. Apartment	FMV	$650,000
	Mortgage	$340,000
	Equity	$310,000
	Total	$690,000

2. Liquid Assets

a. Cash in bank accounts	$126,000
b. Stock in brokerage account	$190,000

3. Total Assets at Separation $1,006,000

II. Liabilities $0
The Martins have no debt other than mortgages and current bills

III. Net Worth

Net worth before separation $1,006,000

2

TACTIC II
We've got the judge

How Tactic II is executed, and its intended effect

NO matter what actually happened, Bleedem would find an excuse to haul Joe before a judge over something. The deadline for the surrender of the key created a pretense for seeking "temporary relief" from the court over a matter of Mary's personal security.

Hoping the key would not arrive at his office before the Monday deadline, Bleedem had the Notice of Motion and supporting documents prepared for filing as soon as the court was open for business on Monday morning.

Bleedem arranged to have his "operative," Jay Edgar, surprise Joe at school with the delivery of a set of court papers. Jay Edgar, wearing a full lawyer's costume with three-piece suit, white starched shirt and red necktie, made the "service" with a flare. The effect was to double Joe's anxiety and confusion.

The papers told Joe that in three weeks there would be a hearing on Bleedem's request for an order directing Joe to turn over the keys and to stay away from the house until the divorce has been completed.

Mary didn't tell Bleedem that she was afraid of Joe (because she wasn't afraid of him), and she didn't need a court order to keep him away. Joe invaded her privacy because he hadn't known any better. He was not a stalker. She could ensure the same thing didn't happen again by having the locks changed.

Mary's security was not the reason for the hearing. Bleedem was confident Joe would be ordered to turn over the key. The purpose of the request demanding a "stay-away order" was to humiliate and demean Joe, which made it unlikely that Joe would agree to everything requested, and that insured the necessity of a court hearing.

Bleedem's reason for scheduling a hearing on an issue he knew he would win was to demonstrate to Joe that Bleedem could subject him to the power of the court whenever he wanted to. The hearing also created the possibility that the judge might either overreact to or misunderstand the evidence. If the overreaction was at the expense of the other party the effect would be demoralization caused by the belief that the "judge is against me." If the judge misunderstood the evidence, regardless of who prevailed, the message was that the court process was irrational and outcomes were unpredictable. Notice that Bleedem didn't allow his own client to be exposed to any part of this experience. She never saw the Slimeball or the pleadings used to initiate this first hearing.

For the effect Bleedem intended, he had to prevail on at least one issue, but he didn't care which one. He had been well paid for preparing the documentation; it was immaterial whether the money came from Mary or from Joe.

Having court papers delivered to Joe at his classroom by a man dressed in a business suit inflated the seriousness of what was happening, and for him the encounter was disconcerting and somewhat frightening, as Bleedem intended.

By the time he got to the first meeting with his own lawyer, Allen Goode, Joe had been stewing about his "trouble with the court" for three days. He was relieved by Goode's immediate disgust over the Slimeball letter. Goode told Joe that Bleedem was blowing the matter way out proportion for cheap and illusory tactical advantage. Joe heard the reassurance, but he couldn't easily dismiss what Bleedem had done. "Surely," thought Joe innocently, "an adult professional wouldn't go to so much trouble just to mess with my mind." In addition to generating his own fees, messing with Joe's mind was exactly what Bleedem was doing. Underestimating Bleedem's perfidy was an error made by Joe and Goode during the entire case, while ignorance of her own lawyer's activities was Mary's mistake.

The saga of the Martin divorce continues

A fresh set of documents were filed with the court early in the week. Bleedem employed his "operative," Jay Edgar, to serve Joe with the court papers. Edgar had been disbarred for multiple instances of inappropriate physical activities with thirteen different clients during the course of representation, but he still had his lawyer's wardrobe and knew how to wear it without looking like someone in disguise.

When Edgar went to Joe's school he didn't check at the office as a sign directed but instead found Joe's classroom by asking teachers for directions. He needed directions, but he also wanted his presence at school to be noticed so it would be the stuff of embarrassing rumor and gossip. He opened the door, gained Joe's attention, and jerked his head as though he could order Joe to leave his classroom. As soon as Joe was in the hall Jay Edgar asked ominously, "Are you Joe Martin?" Joe said something approximating the word "Yes," and Edgar handed him an envelope, saying dramatically, "Joe Martin, you have been served."

It was the same kind of envelope the Slimeball came in. Joe noticed a tremor in his hand.

He called the office to get another teacher to stand in for him. Then he went home and took to his bed.

The next day, Joe stood in front of his closet for a half-hour before he could choose what to wear. He knew lawyers wore neckties so he decided to wear one too, even though all of his dress shirts were tight at the collar, which restricted the flow of blood through the carotid artery to his brain. With a little effort he was able to button his shirt; Mary was right, he had gained weight. He noticed the flesh that was squeezed out of the top of his collar, but he made a deliberate decision to not buy a dress shirt that fit, reasoning that the number of times he would have to wear a tie would be minimal and not worth the cost of a new shirt. Since he "wasn't the kind of guy who wears a tie" the idea of buying a shirt that fit to wear when doing stressful legal work had never occurred to him.

Joe read the papers before he left for Goode's office. Bleedem and Mary were asking a judge to order:

- Joe to surrender to Bleedem all house keys in his possession or under his control.

- That Joe be excluded from the family home and ordered to stay 100 feet away from the house unless he first obtained Mary's permission to visit at a specific time and date.

- Joe to pay Bleedem & Bleedem a fee to compensate for the expense of this "unnecessary hearing."

Joe's second meeting with Allen Goode; Goode speaks, but can Joe hear?

Joe was impressed with Allen Goode's professional cool and the disdain he showed for George Bleedem and Bleedem's tactics. Goode said plainly, "People need time to grieve during a divorce. Lawyers should leave them alone for as long as it takes to make their own division by two."

Goode said lawyers like Bleedem were predators and parasites, which was something Joe liked to hear at first. But the more he thought about the statement, the less solace it provided. If Bleedem was a predator and a parasite, *who* was his victim?

Goode went on to say, "As the case progresses you are likely to find you can't think of a reason for Bleedem's legal maneuvers. Add confusion to the other normal intense emotional experiences and you might feel insane. Use this 'heuristic' or rule-of-thumb: The first, best, and most likely explanation for anything Bleedem does is generation of income for himself. If that fits, no further analysis is necessary."

Goode explained that while they were despicable and repulsive, lawyers like Bleedem were on the safe side of what lawyers were allowed to do. Rules of Professional Conduct were created for application to civil cases where the parties are legal "strangers" to each other, and it makes sense to require lawyers to provide "vigorous" or even "zealous" representation.

But these requirements become destructive when applied to divorce cases where the relationship between the parties is or was intimate. Very few divorces require the vigorous or zealous attention of lawyers. (In many jurisdictions less than three percent of the divorcing population requires a trial on even a single issue. For example, see the county-by-county statistics maintained for the last fifteen years by the California Administrative Office of the Courts.) There are even fewer spouses who deserve to be the targets of these lawyers. But that's what one gets if unfortunate enough to have a spouse who hires a lawyer like Bleedem, whether intentionally or negligently.

Goode told Joe that lawyers like Bleedem are extremely effective in generating fees for themselves and in demoralizing the opposition. The torment continues until complete capitulation or until the client runs out of money.

Joe said that Mary had withdrawn $25,000 from their bank account. Goode said that he'd need a check in the same amount and that would be just the beginning of the payments Joe would have to make.

Goode looked at Bleedem's motion and said it was a stupid waste of time and money unless Joe was still unwilling to give up the key. Joe told him about the personal Stuff in the shop, and he was unsettled when

Goode explained that, by making an issue over removing "Stuff," he had probably made Bleedem determined to find out what it was.

Joe told Goode what the "Stuff" was, and Goode understood why he wanted to get it out of the house, but he didn't understand why Joe hadn't taken it with him when he moved into the apartment.

Goode next studied the Slimeball [letter] and explained that it was a particularly virulent version of a template floating between law offices for as long as he had been in practice.

Goode explained to Joe, "I can provide only limited protection against a 'tire-biter' like Bleedem. They are too difficult for judges to handle. The judge just wants cases like these and the lawyers involved in them to get out of the courtroom. In the judge's eyes, I'm likely to be seen as being just as unethical as Bleedem no matter how careful I am to be beyond reproach.

"And Joe," Goode continued, "make no mistake about it, I'll give you my best, but I'll never stoop to Bleedem's level. Not for you or for anyone else. It may sound righteous, but I'm not doing things I know to be wrong and immoral. Even if I were willing, fighting fire with fire won't work for you. Joe, you are in a very bad situation. You would be treated far more decently if you were accused of a crime."

"What's a tire-biter?" Joe asked.

"A tire-biter is a lawyer who, for a substantial fee, will infuse your family with his own family's problems, and who is so mean that he will bite the tires of a moving car."

"Why is this happening to me?" Joe whined.

"Joe, listen. I don't know why it's happening to you. I hope you'll think about why you asked that question: it suggests that you have unrealistic expectations of what I can do as your lawyer. But you asked, so I'll tell you what I've discovered about myself. All forms of the 'Why me?' question are immature, self-indulgent and useless. I'll be interested to see, at the end of your case, if you agree with me.

"Also, remember that I didn't pick your wife, and I didn't pick her lawyer."

Goode had two recommendations for Joe.

"First, give me your copy of the Slimeball so that you won't have it to obsess over. Second, I recommend that you don't attend the hearing on the motion."

Utterly ignoring his lawyer's first offered advice, Joe said that he wanted to keep the Slimeball, and that he intended to go to the hearing.

Court

The hearing was set for 8:30 AM. Joe was waiting at the courtroom doors when they opened at 8:15. At 8:30 Goode was not there. By 8:40, the judge had not yet taken the bench, and Goode was still not there. Joe was on the verge of panic when the judge and Goode entered the courtroom at 8:45.

Mary did not attend.

When the case was finally called at 11:15, the judge, a woman in her fifties, said she had read the file and was prepared to rule. Both lawyers said, "Submitted." The judge granted the motion in all of its particulars.

The judge concluded her order with special words for Joe:

"Do you understand that I am allowing you to get your Stuff out of the house, but it will be under supervision. Thereafter you are prohibited from going to the house unless invited by Mary Martin. The invitation must be initiated by her. You are prohibited from calling her by telephone. Do you understand me, Mr. Martin?"

Joe said he did.

"What does 'prohibit' mean Mr. Martin?"

Joe was taken by surprise. This was something he might require a student to do. He needed two starts before he could make a coherent statement: "I am not supposed to do it."

The judge went on … and then she went off – on him:

"Mr. Martin, this case shouldn't have been on my docket today. It shouldn't have been on any judge's docket. You could have avoided it by giving the key to Ms. Martin when you moved to the apartment. That's what you should have done. You had another chance to give it to Mr. Bleedem, but you didn't. This Court is not to be trifled with. To help you understand what I mean by that, I order you to pay $5,000 in fees to Mr. Bleedem's office to be credited to Ms. Martin's account. Mr. Martin, you shall deliver a $5,000 cashier's check to Mr. Bleedem's office before the close of business – 5 PM – today. Mr. Bleedem, you will prepare the Order. Next case."

George Bleedem felt like he had hit a grand slam when he left the courtroom. Joe felt as though his head had been a ball hit by Bleedem's bat.

Joe also decided that he would never again make a student define a common word in the classroom in order to make a point. He never intentionally used humiliation as a teaching technique, but in the future he would be far more careful to avoid accidental or incidental humiliation.

Supplemental Material for Chapter 2:

Appendices II, III, IV, V, starting on page 89.

3

TACTIC III
Demand, invade, warn, accuse
The 1-2-3 punch combination

How Tactic III is implemented and its intended effect

In boxing, various kinds of punches are identified by number. An important part of a boxer's training is to learn to deliver several punches in quick succession. For a right-handed fighter, punch #1 is a "Left Jab," a short poke with the left arm. The #2 punch is a "Right Cross," a power punch delivered with body weight behind it. Punch #3 is a "Left Hook," which is a semi-circular punch aimed at the right side of the head.

Bleedem initiated three actions aimed at Joe. Each one of them alone would have had limited effect, but the quick combination created a cumulative impact greater than the sum of the damage possible from each move made separately.

The Left Jab was Bleedem's letter saying, in effect, "You better get your work done on time, because there will be no extensions." It was vaguely insulting because no extension has been requested. It was vaguely threatening because it said that Bleedem wouldn't cut any slack if a request were made for additional time to complete the collection, organization and assembly of the information he's demanded.

The Right Cross was the most powerful of the three moves and consisted of a second appeal to the court. This time Bleedem complains that the work Joe finished just under the deadline was incomplete and poorly done. He asked for an order forcing Joe to do it correctly. The blow came in the form of the statement Bleedem filed with the court. He maintained that the inadequacy of the work Joe had done, combined with the fact that Joe handled the finances for 17 years, added up to suggest that the material missing from Joe's work could have been an attempt to hide something from Ms. Martin, her attorney, and, ultimately, the court itself.

The Left Hook was the personal delivery to Joe of the order from the first hearing by the invasive and spooky Jay Edgar.

What it does

The Left Jab was annoying and reminded Joe that, at this time in his life, there will be no "business as usual." Joe got a letter telling him, in advance, that he'd better not screw-up. This was not something he was accustomed to. Aside from his marriage, Joe assumed that when he tried to do something he would get it right. The Right Cross, the innuendo contained in the motion to compel discovery, hurt because Bleedem came very close to calling Joe a crook. Joe thought he was going to get a divorce; now he's wondering if he's going to jail for something he didn't do. The Left Hook would have had little effect if Joe wasn't already shaken, and if he had not already encountered the creepy Jay Edgar. This second encounter with Bleedem in the form of Edgar made Joe feel as though Bleedem were omniscient.

Joe's demoralization was reaching completion. Goode realized this and attempted to protect Joe by showing the court that Bleedem was a bully, but such a demonstration would be risky. If a judge didn't understand that bullying can take place outside the courtroom, and that only she can do anything about it, the attempt to report it would sound like tattling or whining. Goode's attempted intervention was likely to boomerang when Bleedem characterized the complaints against him as "a paltry attempt to distract the court's attention away from Mr. Martin, who has just provided the court with an indicator of his determination to hide something."

Joe moves his Stuff

An appointment was made for the night after the hearing for Joe to remove his Stuff from his shop. Since he didn't know if he would ever have access to it again, he decided to take his tools and all the material and equipment he had accumulated while working on the Gizmo. It would be too much to put into his car, so he asked Frank Meredith, another teacher at school, if he could bring his pick-up and help out.

Joe didn't like Meredith, who he considered a toady, but he didn't know anyone else with a truck. When they arrived at the house, Mary was not there but Jay Edgar was waiting to greet them.

Once in the shop, Joe picked up a box with his Stuff in it and almost made it to the door before Jay Edgar stopped him. Edgar explained he was under a court order to inventory everything that left the house. Joe, desperate, said, "Okay, this is a box full of Hustler magazines. Just write down that it was a box of magazines; no one, especially Mary, needs to know about them."

Edgar grinned, "I've got to get instructions from Bleedem. He's going to love this."

The instructions were to keep the box in the house until a photographer got there. When the photographer arrived, he helped Edgar spread what turned out to be sixteen issues of Hustler magazine around on the floor so they could be photographed individually and collectively. They opened every magazine to a particularly graphic photograph and added those to the photographic record. Edgar and the photographer were gleeful as they did their work. Joe was sick. Frank Meredith thought about how he'd tell the story to the other teachers.

Mary had decided to be away from the house when Joe came for his Stuff. She returned after two hours and was surprised to find that Jay Edgar, a photographer, Frank Meredith, and Joe were still there. Then she saw the copies of Hustler spread out on the living room floor. She was mortified by the fact that the magazines were in her house and more so that these strangers had found out about them. She felt like running away, but it was her house, so she went to her bedroom and stayed there until Jay Edgar called out to say he was leaving.

Two weeks went by. Joe remained in a daze from the thumping he'd taken. The story of the magazines went through the school faculty by noon the day after it happened. Joe should have rented his own truck.

Joe was drinking more beer than usual. He got a letter from Goode saying that it was time to prepare the Comprehensive Financial Statement required by statute. It was due in two weeks, but he would ask Bleedem for an extra thirty days, which is customarily granted.

Joe understood the letter to mean that he had six-weeks to complete the project, so he put it out of his mind.

Goode called Joe to tell him that his request for the thirty-day extension had been denied. Joe had thirteen days to put together a Comprehensive

Financial Statement. Goode acknowledged that it's not something anyone wants to do and that Joe probably thinks he can't do it. Goode said that such feelings are typical for everyone during the first several months of a divorce. The law may have been written by people who had never had the experience and didn't know how debilitating it was, but the work still had to be done.

The **Left Jab** came on the day after this phone conversation. It was a letter from Bleedem saying that, because Joe has had exclusive control of the joint finances for so long, Bleedem thought it important to get a description of all existing property as soon as possible. This would allow less time for "assets to disappear." Bleedem said he was not accusing Joe of anything and was merely trying to limit the window of opportunity for "possible mischief."

He ended the letter by saying that if the Comprehensive Financial Statement had not been delivered to his office on the day it was due, he would file another motion with the court. This motion would seek an order compelling Joe to produce the Financial Statement, and it would, once again, request an award of fees. He enclosed a completed draft of the motion, to show it was ready and could be filed on the day the deadline was missed. [When a lawyer writes a letter making a demand, it is appropriate and effective to complete and enclose the expensive paperwork required to ask a court to compel the action the letter demands. This also means the lawyer making the demand is willing to spend the time on work that may be unnecessary.]

Goode recognized this **Jab** for the cheap and weak punch that it was. He also realized that Joe would believe every word of it, and he would consider himself accused of the theft of property that wasn't missing.

He made a decision not to share the threat and innuendo with Joe. He wrote a brief letter to Joe saying that Bleedem had confirmed in writing his refusal to grant an extension. Therefore, the Financial Statement had to be done by the deadline.

Joe worked hard and inefficiently to get the Financial Statement prepared on time. He delivered it to Bleedem's office at 4:55 PM on the day it was due.

Bleedem was disappointed that the Financial Statement came in before the deadline. If it had been late, he could have filed the motion without changing the paperwork. Nevertheless, he had saved the next morning to do a second draft; he was confident that the Financial Statement would be, in at least some respects, incomplete. No matter how well Joe had done the job, something would be missing, because something was always missing. Bleedem had to find it and then he could ask the court to order Joe to do all of the work required by Bleedem's discovery demands. It was nothing but another excuse to haul Joe in front of a judge.

When he looked through Joe's Financial Statement, Bleedem was amused. Joe claimed that some of the missing documents were in the house. Joe couldn't go to the house without Mary's permission, and he had been ordered not to call her, so he couldn't get the paperwork. He said that he'd finish the Financial Statement when he was given permission to re-enter the house.

It was literally true, but the court may or may not see it as an excuse. Bleedem argued that if contacted he would have arranged for Joe to go to the house, so Joe's claim was nothing but a ploy. Bleedem didn't care. He was pleased to have grounds to file another motion so close in time to the first. In the motion, Bleedem demanded the missing material and called Joe's excuse "an attempt to deceive and frustrate the course of justice. If the missing documents were truly in the house, Respondent could have made arrangements through his lawyer to get them." [Of course Joe couldn't call Bleedem directly. So he would have had to call Goode who would call Bleedem who would call Mary and then call Goode who would then call Joe, who was only five telephone calls away from getting access to his own house.]

Now The **Right Cross** connected when Bleedem added his riff about how Mary *never had an opportunity* to manage finances during 17 years of marriage; Bleedem said he was concerned about Joe's accountability ever since he refused to turn over the key to the house. That was why he insisted on prompt compliance within statutory time limits. Joe was holding off a full accounting, and one could only guess why.

Goode decided that to protect Joe's morale, an effort had to be made to expose Bleedem for what he was.

He called Joe to his office and explained what had happened. Goode said he would make a major effort to expose Bleedem and his bullying tactics. If the judge understood how Bleedem practices, the momentum of the case would shift. However, there is a chance the judge won't understand what Goode is trying to describe. She might conclude that, of the two lawyers, it is Goode who is the worst because he had gone to a lot of trouble and expense to tattle to the court about insignificant things.

Goode concluded his "Memorandum of Points and Authorities" by describing the case as the termination of a long marriage between two school teachers who saved and invested well and who now need to divide their property by two, which they should be able to do as well or better than two lawyers.

Goode couldn't resist ending his argument with a joke of his own creation. He wrote, "Of course, all divorce attorneys can divide by two. The problem is that we get different answers and then argue about arithmetic."

Joe got a copy of Goode's Memorandum of Points and Authorities, which consisted of twenty printed pages, plus five Appendices of various tables. All of it is written under the title: "Legal Bullying in Family Law Cases."

Goode had attempted to demonstrate how a series of acts not worth reacting to could have a serious cumulative effect, especially in the first stages of divorce when each party is emotionally raw and vulnerable.

Goode explained what most schools and labor law have finally figured out: Bullying can only take place when the bully and the target are in a system from which the victim cannot escape and in which the victim cannot retaliate with overwhelming force. The only source of relief the victim can appeal to is the authority that legitimately dominates the system. If it is the legal system, judges have the power to eliminate bullying. If they choose to ignore it when it is brought to their attention (on the grounds that the complaint is sniveling or that it came from a whiner or a tattletale), their authority becomes complicit in the bullying – and the judge becomes an essential participant in systematic torment.

Would the court get it or would it be insulted? Joe wondered. Goode knows the judge might not take the time to read it, but he said, "It has to be written. It can't be explained in the minute or two you have to speak at a hearing."

A weak **Left Hook** came the day before the hearing on Bleedem's second motion. Jay Edgar returned to Joe's classroom to deliver a copy of the written order from the first hearing. Edgar said in his scariest voice: "Joseph Martin, you have been served."

To enforce a court order by contempt, it must be proven that the person to whom the order was directed had personal knowledge of its content. The best evidence is proof that a copy of the order was personally served, so there was theoretical justification for serving Joe at school and what Bleedem has done is not "unethical." However, Joe was in court when the order was made, and the judge questioned him to make sure he understood. Therefore, a hearing transcript could prove Joe knew the content of the order. Personal service was not improper, but it wasn't necessary. The real purpose was to allow Jay Edgar to once again get into Joe's face to spook him and to contribute to Joe's long-term demoralization.

When it was finally heard, Goode's motion failed and the judge denied Joe's request for attorneys' fees. Then, she turned her attention to Goode personally. It was his day in the barrel, and while he didn't protect Joe, he served as a diversion. The judge didn't appreciate Goode's work on bullying and obviously didn't understand it. She berated Goode for expecting the court to read such an "irrelevant rant," for "forcing Mr. Bleedem to spend time trying to figure out what you were trying to say," and for "wasting your time and, presumably, your client's money." Looking at Joe she said, "I order you to pay Mr. Bleedem $1,000 to compensate him for the time he had to spend trying to deal with this Thing your lawyer wrote. Get the money to him by cashier's check by close of business today. And, Mr. Martin, I hope Mr. Goode doesn't bill you for the time he wasted."

Goode said nothing. It had been another bad day in court.

Supplemental Material for Chapter 3:

Appendices I, II, III, IV, and V, starting on page 87.

4

TACTIC IV
Words will never hurt you, or do they?

How Tactic IV is executed and what it does

Joe was going to be bombarded with a set of written questions, called "Interrogatories," to which he would have to provide written answers under oath.

By now Joe feared that, no matter what he did, Bleedem would claim it was inadequate and also evidence of criminal conduct. Joe felt like he was staggering.

Goode wasn't doing too well himself after being slapped down for his attempt to demonstrate Bleedem's bullying. He prepared a "Motion for a Protective Order" to combat Bleedem's "Motion to Compel."

Bleedem and Goode were now going at it. The two lawyers were settling into "discovery litigation" which created a "case within the case" of what could have been a simple divorce.

Joe's bashing as a result of Tactic III, the 1-2-3 Punch Combination, led to some unfortunate thinking. Instead of attending to the questions being asked in the Interrogatories, he got obsessed by how the Enron case demonstrated that he had been right when he had said that investing in the stock market was foolish because only insiders had the information necessary to properly analyze the value of stock. This occurred to him as a justification for the casual way he had invested joint funds. Somehow, he didn't see the clear implication of these statements, which would be: "If you concluded that the Enron debacle proved that investment in the stock market is an irrational act, why did you leave joint funds in the market after you had this realization?"

There was no good answer to that question, so if Joe sounded off about Enron in response to the "discovery demand," he would be serving up his own head to Bleedem on a platter.

Joe and the "Interrogatories"

The second trip to the house for the collection of business documents was uneventful. Joe was selective about what he retained. It was well organized and easy to locate. He was done and the inventory completed in less than an hour.

One full day passed without being reminded of his divorce, but that's all. When Joe got back to the apartment after school, there was a voicemail message asking him to call Goode. Goode explained that he had just received a hundred pages of questions known as "Interrogatories," which had to be answered within the next thirty days. Given previous experience, Goode said they could expect no extension of that deadline.

The box below is included to give the reader a low level experience similar to Joe's intense experience. You are likely to be repulsed by the legal language; it's intensive so we keep it brief. We strongly recommend that you read it aloud even if there is no one to listen. Then read aloud the paragraph that describes what Joe would have to do to comply with the legal demands imposed on him by what he's just received.

When Joe got the Bundle from Goode he read the first six questions aloud:

> 1. Please list each and every stock or bond purchase or sale you have made since the date of marriage. Identify the security, the transaction date, the purchase or sale amount, the name, address and phone number of the broker handling the same.
>
> *[On average Joe sold shares of stock twice a year and purchased stock twice a year. This means that this list should include about four transactions each, for seventeen years of marriage (68 transactions).]*
>
> 2. With respect to the list of transactions prepared in response to Interrogatory I (Set 1), please explain your reason(s) for completing each of those transactions.
>
> 3. With respect to the transactions listed in your answer to Interrogatory I (Set 1), please describe how you satisfied your Fiduciary Duty to the Petitioner Mary Martin when making the decision to buy or sell each security.

4. With respect to Interrogatory 1 (Set 1), please identify each and every document considered by you in making the decisions to buy or sell each security. Describe said documents with their current location and with the specificity necessary for the preparation of a formal Demand for Document Production [which will be completed and served upon receipt of your response to these Interrogatories].

5. With respect to each transaction listed in response to Interrogatory 1 (Set 1), please describe each and every conversation with any person having an effect on your decision to buy or sell each security. Please indicate the name of the person with whom you conversed, the date of the conversation, the location of the conversation, the gist of the conversation, and the current address and telephone number of each person you have identified.

6. With respect to each transaction listed in response to Interrogatory 1 (Set 1), describe the date, place and gist of every conversation you had with Petitioner Mary Martin about each transaction.

How do you feel after reading these 309 words? Joe's reaction is described below; there is more information about interrogatories at the conclusion of the chapter.

Joe didn't understand why he was being asked most of the questions that followed. They asked about foreign bank accounts (he had none) and expenditures for gifts to or recreational activities (including hotel and motel rooms) with women other than Mary Martin (none). There were also lots of questions about the apartment and why he bought it in his name only.

He didn't have most of the documents he was supposed to identify. He was getting to know Bleedem so well that he could predict what was coming next. If he didn't identify documents Bleedem would say he was being uncooperative or that he was hiding evidence. Then, Bleedem would say that the absence of documentation was evidence of failure to meet the Fiduciary Duty.

Joe left the questions in the envelope for a week, but was abruptly reminded of them when Jay Edgar rang his doorbell at 9 PM to deliver the written order from the second hearing. (This was the hearing where Joe was required to pay Bleedem for the time it took him to read the material submitted by Goode on Joe's behalf. The personal delivery of the documents was unnecessary because there had been complete compliance with everything the judge directed, so Bleedem is close to violation of the Rule that prohibits one attorney to make direct contact with another attorney's client.) To Joe, it's another instance where his lawyer didn't "protect him."

Joe had tax returns for seventeen years and the year-end brokerage statements to identify all of his trades, which didn't amount to more than seven or eight a year (for a total of 150 transactions). Summarizing the details was tedious but required nothing more than copying information. What he relied on to make each purchase or sale was problematic. He hadn't retained any written information. Why buy? Why sell? He didn't know. He'd see something in the newspaper or on TV and he'd act. He never risked more than he thought they could lose.

He had been a poor investor. He didn't really know what he was doing. When the Enron scandal broke, his worst suspicions were confirmed. The company's public financial statements were fiction even though they had been approved by one of the biggest accounting firms in the world. The accountants were being paid so much to do the complicated audit that they feared they would lose the work if they said anything negative about the company employing them.

So, unless you had illegal information from an inside source, as lots of people surely did, it was like betting on a fixed prizefight without knowing which fighter was going to take the fall. Did he stop investing? No. He left nearly half their liquid assets in the market. He had made one series of purchases that more than made up for their losses. He had always liked Apple computers and had owned several. Whenever Apple introduced a new product and Joe liked the way it looked, he would purchase another hundred shares of Apple stock. That was the way he satisfied his fiduciary duty to Mary. Was he going to get creamed?

Maybe not. Goode explained that the Fiduciary Duty between spouses isn't like the one owed to customers by certain businesses. When lawyers hold money in trust, for example, they had better be able to point to the account in which it's held. They should be able to show their books and the bank's books reconciled from the day of the first deposit onward –

and the money had better be absolutely safe.

In contrast, partners and spouses may not do reckless things with joint money. Beyond that, there are two essential duties: one can't use joint funds in a way that benefits his own interests over the interests of the partner, and both partners have to have full access to the accounting records of the partnership.

After reviewing a draft of Joe's answers, Goode decided to be pro-active and to seek some of the protection Joe seemed to want. Before the compliance deadline, he filed a motion asking for a "protective order" that allowed Joe to disregard most of the Interrogatories on the grounds that they had been prepared like a shotgun shell. Bleedem wasn't looking for anything specific. Instead, he was asking every question that had ever appeared on any set of Interrogatories that had ever passed through his office.

The hearing on Goode's "motion for a protective order" was scheduled after the deadline for answers. When the deadline came and went, Bleedem filed a "motion to compel" answers to all the questions. Of course, both sides asked for an order requiring the other to pay attorney's fees.

The third hearing was a non-event. It was held before the same judge, who was having none of it. She told the lawyers she wasn't going to spend the time studying nearly two hundred questions (about a case she knew little about) in order to decide which questions Mr. Martin would or would not have to answer. She asked Goode if Mr. Martin had answered any of the questions. Goode said that he had. She ordered those answers to be delivered to Bleedem's office before the close of business that afternoon.

Joe felt relieved.

She continued (postponed) the hearing for sixty days and told the lawyers to be professional and resolve at least something between themselves. She told them that if they were back in court in sixty days with the same problem, her ruling would be essentially the same. She wouldn't study a single question. Instead she would appoint a lawyer ["Special Master"] to do the work for them; the only question she'd decide would be which side would pay the Special Master.

Perhaps the most important feature of this hearing was something that no one expected. Mary was present and for the first time she got a sense of what was really happening in her case. Mary was confused and didn't know what the hearing was all about. Was it her case? Of course it was, but it didn't sound like it. In her state of confusion and consternation she didn't want to talk to Bleedem because she feared he would be condescending and patronizing without realizing what he was doing. She didn't want Joe to know she had been present when he suffered this loss, for whatever he did that the judge didn't like.

ENDNOTE #1 – More About Interrogatories

The timing of the delivery of the Interrogatories confirms Joe's sense of how relentless the process will continue to be. The demand for a long list with lots of details is often overwhelming for someone who is still raw from the separation and suffering of the early phases of divorce.

Note that while the Interrogatories originate with Mary's lawyer Bleedem, Joe receives the documents from his lawyer with instructions to answer in 30 days. The process is set up so that it's your own lawyer who insists that you do this pointless and exhausting work.

Other annoying and demoralizing aspects of the Interrogatories include:

- Continuing use of the set number. If this is Set 1, how many more sets will there be? Some jurisdictions require the inclusion of the set number, but required or not it is still subtly discouraging.

- Capitalization of the first letters in the term Fiduciary Duty, which makes the principle sound far more ominous than it really is.

- Reference to Mary as "Petitioner Mary Martin" is unnecessary, but it emphasizes the dehumanization that comes with the judicial process.

The purpose is rarely the collection of valuable information. The point is to overwhelm the victim with little digs, such as when a dirty boxer rubs or whips the rough surface made by the laces on the inside of his gloves across his opponent's eyebrow. This is done to open a cut. Even a small cut on the face will bleed heavily enough to interfere with vision.

A "cut man" in the corner can almost always stop the bleeding in the one-minute break between rounds but, once the next round begins, the opponent will aim for the cut knowing that a direct hit will open it. This will either obscure vision, making it easier to land an unanticipated punch from the side, or it can cause the fight to be stopped with a technical knock out.

This is similar to what's happening to Joe. The pointless questions keep coming and coming, and they create a space where he thinks about the problems his answers may cause. Was he irresponsible with the investment of joint funds? He's beginning to believe that he was. Maybe he should be held responsible for the losses. He could accept that, but what about premature sales? Will Bleedem question him for selling stock that increased in value, as well as the loss when a stock they owned decreased in value? How could he compensate Mary for that? How could it be measured?

By now he has no illusions about seeking protection from the court, and he is somewhat surprised that Goode wanted to file the motion for a protective order against frivolous interrogatories. "Maybe he needs the money," thought Joe.

Jay Edgar's appearance at his apartment that night was unsettling but, for the time being, the effect on Joe is uncertain.

Nothing particularly dramatic happened in this round, but Bleedem is moving the inside of his boxing gloves around Joe's eyes, and he's opened up a cut. It is so small that Joe doesn't notice it, but he will.

5

TACTIC V
Hit From Behind. *Who profits?*

How Tactic V is executed

Tactic V is called "Hit From Behind" because Joe was being hit from behind in two different ways. The first was the seizure of his garbage by Jay Edgar on Bleedem's instruction. This was done after Joe deposited garbage and trash on the evening before the deadline for the Document Production. One of the demands had instructed Joe to produce all the pornographic material purchased with joint funds not discovered in Joe's shop at the outset of the case.

Bleedem rationalized the seizure by saying that, by depositing garbage in the can on the very night before the production was to take place, Joe created a reasonable suspicion there was something in the can that could be used as evidence.

The law wasn't clear on whether Jay Edgar could rummage through or move the contents of the can to another location, so Bleedem instructed him to put the can into a big plastic bag and replace it with a new can of equal or greater value.

Bleedem proposed that the contents of the can could be examined in court under judicial supervision.

The second hit originates with Bleedem, but its force is transferred to Joe through his own lawyer. Goode explained, once again, that money generated in the form of fees can usually explain Bleedem's behavior. This time, however, Joe couldn't ignore the observation that Goode's fees were driven by what Bleedem did. Goode acknowledged the truth of Joe's insight and shortly thereafter informed him that his firm needed another check for $25,000.

Bleedem, of course, didn't care about the amount of joint funds used to purchase smut. He played on the issue because he knew it was, understandably, a source of great embarrassment for Joe. It was also useful to "keep the pot stirred" because it provided new material for inclusion in whatever legal brief was being prepared at the time. Referring to a person's "possession of a pornography library" puts that person at a disadvantage when defending against the charge that follows, no matter what that charge happened to be.

The idea of sequestering the garbage can was to generate fees and to add some physical intimidation to the mix. By seizing Joe's garbage can, Bleedem was sending the message: "You'll never know where I'm coming from or what I'm coming after. Even the grounds of your apartment building are not safe from our encroachment." Henceforth, would Joe be able to hear a sound in the vicinity of his garbage can without thinking, "It's them. What have I thrown away since the last pick-up?"

The realization that his own defender was profiting by the campaign against him was devastating. At the outset Joe imagined he could pay an attorney to bring Bleedem to heel, even though Goode carefully explained there was little he could do. Joe didn't fully appreciate the significance of those words at the time, but later he understood them all too well. When Bleedem acted, Goode would react – and they would both make a lot of money to do their dance. For Joe, the dynamic led to this conclusion: What incentive does Goode have to bring this to an end?

The Saga continues:

After the hearing and the delivery of the completed answers, Joe felt he needed and had earned a rest longer than the single day he got after he finished the Comprehensive Financial Statement.

He mentioned to Goode that he dreaded the appearance of Jay Edgar because that would be the harbinger of the Next Bad Thing. Goode explained there was no point in personally delivering a copy of the order to Joe. The order didn't require him to do anything (or refrain from doing something), and delivering it in person seemed too close to obvious harassment for Bleedem to risk; he was safe from Jay Edgar for the moment.

Goode qualified the reassurance by adding that Bleedem could start the next round of "discovery" the following day.

That was what Bleedem did. The principal investigative tools used in civil litigation are Interrogatories (written questions to be answered under oath), Demand for the Production of Documents (that are or may be relevant to the case), and Deposition (which is a way either side can require anyone to take an oath and answer questions about what they know that might have bearing on the case).

Joe told Goode that although he had records of the stock trades, there were no backup files to support his decisions to buy or sell – and he had no recollection of conversations with anyone about those decisions. So that was easy; maybe it cooked his goose on the fiduciary thing, but there it was.

Goode explained that the fiduciary duty between spouses prohibited unfair dealings with each other, withholding of financial records, and reckless use of joint funds. None of those things occurred in this marriage, so that wasn't a true issue. But nothing raised so far was a true issue. Everything Bleedem had done was first to generate fees for himself and then to demoralize Joe to the point where Joe would give in to an unreasonable settlement.

"Ultimately," Goode said, "it's far more about his fees than it is about getting Mary more than she 'should' get."

Without thinking, Joe responded, "Your fees too."

Goode nodded his head and without defensiveness said, "Well, there is that."

There was that – for sure. For the last month and a half Goode's intake of revenue for the firm was double what was typical for him, and he couldn't help but notice and enjoy the more friendly treatment he was getting from the partners. His income had doubled, but he was fighting a rear-guard action and it did nothing to make Joe's position better than it was when Goode first entered the case.

•••••

The Demand for Production of Documents arrived the next day. The Demand matched the Interrogatories in many ways. There were demands for the documents listed in the answers to the first few Interrogatories dealing with stock and bond transactions. These were followed by dozens of pages of demands for documents related to expenditure of joint funds on other women, Swiss bank accounts and the like, which had obviously come from a commercial template. It was also obvious that no one had taken the time to delete from the template the questions having no relevance to the Martins' case.

Goode told his assistant to mail a copy to Joe immediately and almost put his copy aside for later study. He assumed the balance of the demands would be inapplicable to the case.

It was fortunate that Goode saw the last few items before Joe did. They included demands of the production of such things as "all writings of whatever source and of any kind" relating to the invention-in-progress of the device referred to as "Gizmo," "all pornographic materials purchased with joint funds," "all documentation having to do with the acquisition of a six-unit apartment building with joint assets but held in Joe's name alone," and "any and all documentary evidence of the claim that the financial records concerning joint property were open and available to Mary."

Joe wanted to know what to do.

"You've got no choice," explained Goode, "give him what you've got. Is there more porn?"

"Yea, three or four and they are worse than Hustler. I really meant to toss them after the last fiasco and never got to it. I'll do it now."

Goode said, "No, you can't. Absolutely do not do it. I understand the temptation, but they must go to Bleedem. I don't think I've explained it to you because it's a long conversation, but one reason for extensive but otherwise unnecessary discovery demands is that it is possible to have a rock solid position but lose the case because you haven't complied with the technical requirements of discovery.

"In other words you lose a winning case because of something that has absolutely no direct connection to the facts of the law of the case itself."

"What would happen if the Bundle I delivered didn't have any smut in it?"

"Do not try to outsmart Bleedem on discovery and don't try to get rid of those magazines. I have to sign the reply so, now that I know about them, I would have to disclose that you had them at one time and that I don't know what happened to them."

"Then what happens?"

"I've never had to deal with anything like that. I might be required to withdraw from the case. Bleedem might make a motion to have me recused. Anyway, over the single issue of those four magazines, Bleedem could bleed you and Mary until you were ready to give her anything to get her lawyer off your back. I would understand why you did it and sympathize with you about the consequence, but I couldn't feel sorry for you."

"It's so unfair."

"Do you want to pay me to reply?"

"No, I don't."

Joe went on to say that he could give them a jumbled boxful of Gizmo documents consisting of random notes and a few receipts for small purchases. He had bought the apartment in his name because Mary couldn't be bothered, and the real estate agent told him that if he took title in his name alone it was just for convenience and Mary would still be a half owner. The checkbook, bills and everything else dealing with money had been in the main part of the house for years.

When Joe started to spend more time in the shop, he moved the records and handled the finances from the same desk where he was doing the rest of his work. There were no documents showing that Mary had access because she didn't; she didn't have it because she didn't want it and hadn't asked for it. But if she had asked she could have had whatever she wanted.

All of this found its way into the response to the demands. Typically, the Bundle wouldn't be ready for delivery to Bleedem's office until the last hour.

•••••

On the morning of the last day before the deadline, Goode received a voicemail from the clerk of court at 8:02 AM. He was advised the Court would rule at noon on Bleedem's ex parte request for an order sequestering the garbage can used by Joe at the apartment building. Bleedem was directed to fax the declarations supporting the request to Goode not later than 9 AM.

Sequester a garbage can? The maneuver was so unusual that Goode had Joe contacted at school with instructions to get to the law office as soon as he could and, no matter what, to be at the courthouse no later than 11:55.

See Appendix VI for a detailed account of "The Garbage Can Hearing," page 99.

Goode almost laughed aloud when the judge announced her ruling:

"This situation is novel, and I see no urgency in resolving it. We will put this issue on the same calendar as the motion to compel answers to interrogatories. I'm going to continue both matters for ninety days. At that hearing, if the lawyers haven't completed what I see as their professional duty to their clients, I intend to appoint a Special Master to rule on the interrogatories and to decide the garbage can issue and, if the contents are to be inventoried, the Special Master can do that too.

"In the meantime, that garbage can has to be kept somewhere that's secure, and it is not going to be my courtroom or chambers.

"Mr. Bleedem, you brought the can to the law. You have an office that has a door that must have a lock. If it doesn't have a lock, get one installed today. I am ordering you to keep the can secure and safe until the hearing three months from now.

"You will bring that can to court, and it must still be sealed as it is now. Otherwise, it must not leave your office for the next 90 days. Actually, instead of leaving for his lunch, I'm going to have my clerk for this courtroom figure out a way to impress our stamp to serve as a seal that will have to be broken to open the bag."

It was hardly a victory, but it was, so far, Goode's best day.

In the meantime, Bleedem was satisfied by the fees he would be able to charge to the case. He was also satisfied by demonstrating his power to jerk Joe and Goode to court with only three hours notice. Once back at his office he completed a billing statement and sent it off to Mary. The case was going well, he noted, but the retainer required additional funding for the work to continue at its current pace.

Mary wasn't interested in anything having to do with economics, but she didn't need help to understand the significance of the bill. Bleedem had exhausted two $25,000 retainers and was into a third, which he wanted paid immediately.

She had never spent $50,000 before. She and Joe didn't have $50,000 when they bought their house. She didn't want to spend another $25,000, so she made an appointment to see Bleedem to find out what was requiring so much expensive work.

Supplemental Material for Chapter 5:

Appendix VI, starting from page 99.

6

TACTIC VI
Mary feels the squeeze

This tactic may be the most destructive of all. Bleedem was managing the case to run up his own fees, which also created fees for the opposing side. His ability to continue this kind of representation depended on not upsetting the client. In Chapter 5 Mary was astonished by the size of the bill she received, and in Chapter 4 she made a clandestine visit to the court when a hearing in her case was being held. She was confused by the proceedings, but she didn't want to look to Bleedem for an explanation.

After the garbage can hearing, which she knew nothing about, she thought she was ready to talk to Bleedem about his fees. She made an appointment to see him. She intended to ask him to explain the expenses incurred and the expenses being generated. With his years of experience, Bleedem seemed to answer her questions while withholding information that would alarm her. Bleedem had three principles working in his favor:

(a) Confirmation bias. Once a decision is made, we want to be right, and there is a strong tendency to attend to information supportive of our decision and to avoid or ignore information to the contrary.

(b) Client participation or the opposite, client ignorance. When a client participates in the management of the case, it is relatively easy for a lawyer to co-opt the client so he will believe that the lawyer's decisions are also his own. Where the client remains ignorant of the case – like Mary – she is dependent on the lawyer's version of what has happened.

(c) The resort to fear. "An immediate amputation to save the life," says the surgeon. Of course you don't want an amputation and its necessity isn't clear to you, but you are likely to accept the advice because if you don't, you will be responsible for a death whether or not an amputation would have saved it. So too with any expert including lawyers. You are given expert advice; if you reject it, you take on the responsibility for any adverse outcome.

What Tactic VI does

Bleedem had Mary in a tight hold, possible because she chose to be ignorant about what her lawyer was doing on her behalf and with her authority. After she watched the hearing and had the conversation with Bleedem about the bills, he knew that in time he would have to relax his grip.

Accordingly, he was required to resort to subtlety and to rely on his well-developed sense of timing to spend enough time on the case to justify a bill approximately equal to what was left of her available cash.

One threat to Bleedem's future fees was the possibility that Mary would consult with another lawyer whose evaluation of Bleedem's work might not be charitable. Even more dangerous would be a meeting between Mary and Joe. Thus far it had been easy to keep them apart. The restraining order prohibited direct contact.

Joe didn't know how much Mary knew about what Bleedem was doing to him. Until quite late in the case, such a conversation would have probably gone like this:

Joe starts by saying something to the effect, "Mary. I've just got to tell you what your lawyer is doing to me. He's requiring me to bla, bla, bla and if I don't do exactly what he requires, he takes me to court and tells the judge that he thinks I'm a wife beater who is also a crook. Mary, you know that I'm not a crook."

"I know you aren't a crook Joe, and I've never said you were a wife beater and everyone knows you're an honest guy. But Joe, neither you nor I went to law school. Neither of us could stand being a lawyer. I needed someone to see me through this thing. I got Bleedem, and I'm not going to switch my horse in midstream."

"My lawyer says your lawyer is a shyster and is doing all this crap to generate fees for himself. How did you find that guy."

"Joe, I'm not going to argue about what you say your lawyer has to say about my lawyer. Bleedem is responsible for protecting me. That's his job. If I could do it myself, I would. But I don't know, how so I can't. I don't know what Bleedem needs to do to properly represent me and I don't see that I have a choice. If not Bleedem, who? You? Could you represent my best interests? Would you even want to try? So do us both a favor. Don't tell me I've got a bad lawyer. It doesn't help either one of us."

Mary was convinced that she needed someone to look after her best interests because she didn't know enough to do it herself. In fact, all she needed to know was that both sides get half. If she was going to get her share of the marital property, what was left to know?

If she knew that both she and Joe had been honest with each other for fifteen years (and she did know it), why would either suddenly become dishonest? If the settlement was progressing toward a division that gave her less than half of the marital property, or if she thought she was entitled to more than half, it would be time to consult with a lawyer. But in this case Joe had never claimed that Mary wasn't entitled to half of whatever they had and Mary never thought she was entitled to more than half.

The next step in the discovery process would be to take Joe's deposition, an ordeal for Joe and very expensive for Mary. When the deposition was over, she would have the cash necessary to pay Bleedem's fees and not much more. Bleedem's very last squeeze would depend on being able to settle the case at the same time the bank account balances reached zero.

Mary questions Bleedem about his fees

Mary met with Bleedem to talk about his fees.

At that meeting, Mary quietly voiced her concerns about the expenses she's incurred. What was happening that was so expensive? Did all divorces cost so much?

Bleedem was ready for her. These were the points he made:

"When you sell a house, you pay the real estate agent 6% of the sale price. If you have a million dollar house, you pay a $60,000 fee.

"In a divorce, an entire estate is being divided and part of a lawyer's job is to make sure he has found everything that needs dividing.

"Without counting your pensions, your estate is worth $1 Million; 6% of a million is $60,000, which is what it has cost you to date. If we count the pensions, the estate is worth at least $1.5 Million and 6% of that would be 90,000. So you have to pay another $30,000 before the cost of the case is as much as the cost of selling a house.

"But the equivalency of fees in a divorce and the commission for selling a house doesn't hold up if the divorce is hard. This case is tough largely because we now have very disturbing evidence of the possibility that Joe was planning to or already has stolen joint property from you. There is also evidence suggesting that he was reckless in the management of your joint property. What about the pornography? You did give him your approval to buy it, didn't you? Of course not! We have to determine the extent of his collection of smut so he can be charged for its full value.

"And Mary, listen very carefully to this. I didn't pick your husband and I didn't pick his lawyer, and neither one of them is making this thing easy."

Attorneys' Fees to Date:

The table on the following page shows the legal activities in the left column with estimates of the maximum number of hours Bleedem and Goode could probably get past a Bar Association Fee Arbitration panel. We assume a billing rate of $300 per hour, which is low for work in a medium size city (> 150,000 population) and probably high for smaller cities.

A copy of the entire combined statement is in Appendix VIII, page 110. Also, see Appendix VII: *"How lawyers and law firms make money - A short course,"* page 108.

Description of Services	Bleedem Attorney Services at $300 per hour	Bleedem Legal Assistant at $150 per hour	Goode Attorney Services at $300 per hour	Goode Legal Assistant at $150 per hour
1st conference w/ client (Mary); draft **Petition, Summons** & design **management plan**	6.5	2.5	4.0	2.0
Draft initial letter to opposite party	2.0	0	0	0
Prepare docs for **Temporary Restraining Order (TRO)** re return of key, exclusion from house & attorney fees	8.0	6.0	0	0
Prepare Opposition to TRO			4.0	2.0
Reply to response to Motion for TRO	4.0	4.0	0	0
Review Reply	0	0	1.0	1.0
Prepare for, attend, and follow-up on **Superior Court hearing**	6.0	4.0	6.0	4.0
Draft letter re completion of Comprehensive Financial Statement	2.5	0	0	0
Receive letter re completion | analyze & discuss with client			2.0	0.5
Review & Analyze Comprehensive Financial Statement	6.0	2.0	4.0	2.0
Prepare **Notice of Motion** and supporting documentation re completion of Comprehensive Financial Statement	6.0	2.0	0	0
Prepare Opposition to motion | Investigate circumstance | Confer with client	0	0	6.0	2.0
Prepare for court, **Appear in court** on motion, Follow-up	6.0	2.0	6.0	2.0
Prepare (1) comprehensive set **of Interrogatories**, coordinated with document production & deposition	8.0	12.0	0	0
Receive & review interrogatories, analyze, discuss & deliver to client | Review answers provided	0	0	8.0	12.0
Receive, review, summarize & **analyze** answers to interrogatories	10.0	20.0	0	0
Prepare **Notice of Motion to Compel** answers to interrogatories	6.0	12.0	0	0
Receive motion to compel, prepare Response	0	0	4.0	4.0
Prepare motion re protective order and "bully memo"	0	0	40.0	40.0
Receive and review **Notice of Motion** re protective order *(extensive* supporting documentation)	8.0	4.0	0	0
Prepare **Reply** to Response to motion to compel further answers to interrogatories	5.0	2.0	0	0
Prepare **Response** to motion for protective order	16.0	12.0	0	0
Receive and analyze Response and Reply	0	0	6.0	4.0
Prepare comprehensive **Demand for Documents** (105 items)	6.0	12.0	0	0
Prepare for, attend and follow-up on court hearing	6.0	6.0	6.0	6.0
Review and analyze documents produced	12.0	24.0	0	0
Prepare **Notice of Motion re Production** of documents and supporting documents	6.0	12.0	0	0
Receive & analyze document demand	0	0	4.0	4.0
Organize and arrange surveillance on garbage can	4.0	6.0	0	0
Prepare pleadings for judicially supervised search of garbage can	8.0	3.0	0	0
Prepare Reply to Response to motion for production of documents	6.0	2.0	0	0
Prepare for Court Hearing re production of documents, protective order & supervised search of can	6.0	6.0	6.0	6.0
	125	139	107	91.5
Totals	X $300 = $37,500 +	X $150 = $20,850 = **$58,350 Bleedem**	X $150 = $16,050 +	X $300 = $27,450 = **$43,500 Goode**

Mary Reflects

Mary was glad to get out of Bleedem's office, but not glad about the message he delivered: six percent of your estate, counting the pensions, is $90,000. Because of what Joe has done and because of the way he is fighting Bleedem, the fees are likely to exceed 6%.

Then she realized that Bleedem was talking about her fees. Joe must be paying a lot of money too. If $90,000 was her minimum, Joe might spend that much too. That would be $180,000 to get divorced. It didn't seem possible.

Bleedem said he had evidence that Joe was trying to steal from her. He said the same thing once before, and Mary had not paid much attention to it. Joe wouldn't steal from her or from anyone else. She didn't want to be married to him but not because he was dishonest. She knew he wasn't dishonest, and he didn't care much for money.

He had been secretive about the magazines; was that dishonest? Maybe. But it seemed different than stealing from her. But if Bleedem has evidence, that had to be cleared up. Joe wouldn't want to leave the marriage with a shadow on his honesty, so maybe they both had to pay to get that done. The whole thing was getting crazy.

The dirty magazines – that was another thing. It was so upsetting to see that stuff laid out in her living room. Joe looked sick while the photographer and the detective – or whatever he was – were enjoying themselves. She didn't want to think about it, but the story of Joe being caught with his magazines made the gossip rounds of her school within a week. Even though they were getting divorced, he didn't want her to know about it. That must mean that he still about cared what she thought of him.

There was one other thing. She would never tell anyone and she knew that Joe wouldn't either. They didn't even mention it to their marital counselor. They hadn't been physically intimate for more than a year. That may have been why Joe had the magazines. She didn't want to know about it, but now felt her own lawyer was shoving it into her face.

On that night when he came to the house and he wouldn't give her his key, she thought he was acting like he believed he should be able to come into the house whenever he felt like it. Maybe she had a different reason for getting so upset: What if she had a man in the house? That was absolutely none of Joe's business. That's why she was so mad. But the real reason he wouldn't give her his key was because he had left his magazines behind and wanted to get them out; if she had known they were there, she'd want him to take them out. What a mess. What had that misunderstanding cost in attorneys' fees?

The misunderstanding was the reason the judge prohibited Joe from coming within 100 feet of the house, as though he had been stalking her. He wasn't a stalker; he isn't a stalker. How humiliating it must have been for him when the judge made the orders. Are the prohibitions against coming near the house common? She never said she wanted either of them.

Mary's objections to the fees her case was generating was the first warning to Bleedem that his client was going to start paying attention to what was going on and what it was costing. He was lucky in that he had two other cases he could put a lot of time into. He could afford to put Mary's case aside and let it mellow.

Joe

It had been his worst teaching semester ever. It was not only because of what was happening in the divorce, but because he had lost his sense of timing with his classes. He also felt like he had lost his footing. Physics is a difficult class for most of his students, and Joe usually had a way of smoothing the transitions from one topic to the next.

He didn't care for the other teachers and whenever he saw Frank Meredith, the guy who was solely responsible for the fact that every teacher and every administrator in every local school district knew about his stack of Hustler magazines, he wanted to bite his face off. Yes, bite his face off. Anger.

He rarely thought about Mary. He had been unable to escape the fact that the woman he had been with for seventeen years had put him through five court hearings in less than four months at a cost that must be nearing $50,000. He didn't know her. He was too busy trying to take care of himself to worry much about her, or even to be very angry with her. He did, however, loathe her lawyer. He loathed and he feared him, and although it had been months since Jay Edgar had been around, he dreaded another "service" of court documents.

The garbage can hearing had twice been put off for an additional ninety days. He didn't even go to court the second time because he knew nothing was going to happen. He was particularly inactive. Was he resting? Vacationing? Taking a break in the middle of work? No. It was as though he had a horrible disease that was in remission, but it was a disease that would come back for sure. He was experiencing a remission that could end precipitously and send him right back to hell.

One year later...

Mary didn't call Bleedem. Joe didn't call Goode.

Goode didn't call Bleedem because he couldn't stand the guy. He didn't call Joe because he had a policy of never contacting a divorce client when the case was quiet. Silence usually meant the client was working on the grief that characterizes divorce. Grief includes a period of depression. No one should be forced to work on a divorce while depressed.

Bleedem didn't call Mary until he needed her money. When he did, the show was back on.

Notice of Deposition

Whenever Joe drove up to the apartment, he dreaded collecting his mail. Nothing good would come by mail now or in the foreseeable future.

His fear was well founded. There was an envelope from Goode's firm in the mailbox. Joe tore it open. It was a Notice of Deposition, with a note on a Post-It from Goode. It said, "This is going to be difficult. We need to prepare; call for appointments."

It said appointments. Plural. This was going to be bad.

7

TACTIC VII
The five-day deposition and beyond

How Tactic VII is executed

Joe was forced to sit in the same chair for an indefinite period while the loathsome George Bleedem asked one stupid question after another for days, and Joe never knew how long it would continue.

Due to the duration of the ordeal and the consumption of alcohol, Joe's judgment failed.

During one of the overnight breaks, Joe called Mary, in desperation, to ask that she call off her hound. He didn't care about the restraining order.

During one of the deposition sessions, when asked about his investment philosophy, he pontificated on how the Enron debacle proved that investing in the stock market was irrational. Just as Goode had warned, there was no good answer when Bleedem asked: "So why did you continue to invest joint funds in the stock market?"

When Bleedem got to questions about Joe's "use" of the Hustler magazines, Goode objected, instructed Joe not to answer, and sought to get a protective order. At the same time, Goode requested the court to issue a protective order to bring the deposition to an end.

When the court set a settlement conference date, Bleedem knew the case – and the income stream – was coming to an end. To maintain control over the client and the case, Bleedem prepared, immediately after court, a comprehensive settlement proposal that *he knew Joe would not be able to accept.*

A detailed analysis of the proposal is set out in the next Chapter, starting on page 76, Endnote #1.

What it does

Listening to hours and hours of a barking dog teaches that it is not the bark that's so painful. It is the period of silence between barks – especially those that continue a bit longer than most and create a hope that it is over – that becomes so painful.

Sitting for a five-day deposition and answering one question after another – without knowing the structure of the examination or how long it will continue – has approximately the same effect as listening to a barking dog for the same period of time.

The deponent is likely to let his guard down because of mental exhaustion, to act out in a way that is self-sabotaging, and/or to volunteer information. A deponent who soothes himself between sessions with the consumption of alcohol is more likely to deteriorate than one who doesn't.

After an experience like this, the victim is more likely to make big concessions to avoid a similar experience at a trial.

At this point, the motions to compel testimony (Bleedem's) and for a protective order (Goode's) are more about attorneys' fees than to harass or protect Joe.

The hearing on contempt placed Joe before what has been a fairly hostile court. It should have been a source of horrible anxiety except, by this time, he had been placed on administrative leave, he continued to drink, and he was numb to the psychological battering administered by Bleedem.

The Saga continues:

After enduring a five-day deposition, Joe spent the weekend in an alcoholic haze. Once back at work, he was disoriented from being away from his classes and his hangover. He expected another fatherly chat when summoned by his principal, but he was surprised to find that he was being placed on leave while the consequences of the discovery of Hustler magazines were explored.

The principal said that, regardless of what happened on account of the Hustlers, he was thinking about a longer administrative leave, which might be the beginning of proceedings to terminate Joe's employment with the district. He told Joe to "get help."

Joe went home, popped open a beer and waited for Jay Edgar to arrive. Sure enough, Edgar served Joe with the 'Order to Show Cause' demanding that he tell the court why he should not be held in contempt for calling Mary. He didn't know why he shouldn't be held in contempt, and he didn't care.

As soon as the deposition was over on Friday afternoon, Bleedem prepared a bill to send to Mary with a demand for more money. He took it to the post office so she would get it on Saturday. Bleedem knew the five-day deposition had brought him to the end game. There was not a lot of money left and, to get it, he had to keep the action moving quickly. He knew a time tested and "honored" way to do it.

Mary had grown very uneasy about the way her case was progressing. She was a talker and hung out with other talkers. As she could tell from the stories she heard about other divorces, hers was different. For one thing, none of her divorced friends had accused their husbands of stealing from them. This was disconcerting because Mary knew a few of those husbands and would not have put much past them. And she didn't care much about what Bleedem had told her. She never believed that Joe would want to take something from her.

The contempt hearing and the hearing to decide whether Joe had to testify about the Hustler magazines were set for the same time. The judge was cranky about the Hustlers.

"Mr. Bleedem, I understand this is a divorce where both parties are teachers and there are no children. You deposed the husband for five days and want to further depose him on what he was doing with sixteen copies of Hustler magazine, which you have made a point of mentioning at every hearing in this case whether it was relevant or not. Have I missed something?"

"No, your honor."

"Then, your request for an order compelling testimony is denied."

Bleedem is not deterred for a moment, "The other matter is the charge of contempt for telephoning my client. A copy of your order from sixteen months ago is attached to my declaration in support of the order to show cause. As you will see from the deposition transcript, this contact was especially pernicious because the Respondent attempted to drive a wedge between me and my client to stop the investigation into what he's done with her money during the last seventeen years other than buy an apartment building with their money but in his name alone."

The judge asked, "Is there evidence that he phoned her or went to the house or bothered her in any way since I made the order – other than this call? Mr. Bleedem?"

"There is no such evidence before the court, your Honor."

"I know what's before me, Mr. Bleedem. Is there evidence that's not before me?"

"I'm not in a position to say one way or the other."

"Is your client here? In the back, are you Mary Martin?"

"Yes."

"The first hearing in your case was almost eighteen months ago, and I issued a restraining order prohibiting Mr. Martin from phoning you or going to your house without an invitation. Aside from this phone call, has he made other calls or come to your house or bothered you in any other way?"

"No."

"Do you feel the need for this protective order to remain in place?"

"No. I didn't know it was there to begin with."

"Very well, the OSC re contempt is dismissed – she doesn't need it, and the original order prohibited Mr. Martin from calling Ms. Martin to wheedle from her an invitation to visit the house. The call in question was to complain about lawyers. Having been one myself, I think it an unfortunate conversation topic, but then, Mr. Bleedem, there's the First Amendment to the U.S. Constitution and all that.

"I'm growing weary of this case. Is there any reason why it won't be ready for a settlement conference in four weeks and the trial calendar four weeks after that?"

Both lawyers signify there was not.

"I'll set the settlement conference in Judge Campbell's department and I'll keep the trial for myself, lucky me. Court is adjourned."

Mary walked with Bleedem in the direction of his office and asked a question before he could preempt the conversation.

"How much did that hearing or whatever it's called cost?"

"To whom? Do you mean the cost of the marshal and the clerk, court reporter, judge...?"

"No. What did it cost me?"

"Well there were actually three hearings. It looks like everything is said and done in a minute or two, but a lot of paperwork has to be prepared and filed with the court in order to get those few moments of attention. And the judge, of course, isn't seeing the material for the first time; she reads what's been written about the issue before she takes the bench."

"But what did it cost?"

"Okay, for the hearing on Joe's refusal to answer questions, I had to research the specific provisions of the right code to tell the judge where her authority to make the order comes from. Then I researched the decisional law for similar cases.

"In my write up, or Memorandum of Points and Authorities, I had to summarize the context for his refusal to answer so she could see why the questions were significant. I think I went through three or four drafts of this one because getting the facts and the law just right was tricky.

"On the contempt, I had to go back to find the order and then describe what happened at the deposition. And I had to do a summary of the law, of course. After the paperwork was done – this was a good-sized stack – we filed it with the court and sent a copy to the other side. When I got the response, I drafted and filed a "Reply" to shoot it down.

"Every step is time-consuming, let me try to count the hours – don't hold me to this six and two and three and two and two equals fifteen plus let's say ten for the OSC and the hearing itself. Twenty-five times $300 is what? $7,500, which is right on the money. Any hearing is going to cost between five and ten thousand dollars when all is said and done. Sometimes it's more, but usually between five and ten."

"That cost $7,500!"

"What you see in the courtroom is just the tip of the iceberg."

"It makes me sick. What's next?"

"I'm going to make a written settlement proposal, and we'll see if there's a need to attend the court-sponsored settlement conference. Oh, if there is a settlement conference in court, you'll have to be there – and plan to spend the entire afternoon. Let me warn you that if they don't accept the settlement I'm about to propose, I have to start preparing for trial and that gets very expensive. And there is no choice. If there is a trial, we have to be prepared – and the best way to get a settlement is to prepare for trial. It's as simple as that. No choice."

Bleedem's last sentence is a form of black art. He is warning her about the cost of the trial preparation he will do, to promote settlement. But he can settle the case on terms both reasonable and "fair" without the trial preparation, and as he's spending Mary's money he knows he can settle the case and that the trial he's "preparing" for *will not take place.*

See Chapter 8, Endnote #1, starting at the bottom of page 75, for a copy of the proposal and an analysis of its implicit terms.

8

TACTIC VIII
Squeezing out the last dollar

Time for the Bubble & Squeak*

At the conclusion of the previous episode: a recap

The lawyers appeared back before their judge for another noon hour hearing. Mary, curious about what was going on in her case, got to the courtroom at noon and once again sat in the last row.

The judge denied the request for an order to compel Joe to testify about his use of the Hustler magazines. She asked Mary if Joe had bothered her since the restraining order was made against him 18 months ago. Mary said he hadn't and added that she didn't know anything about a restraining order. The judge ruled that by making one call the night after he had been in deposition all day, his action did not constitute a violation of her restraining order. He was not in contempt of the court. Then she vacated the restraining order in its entirety.

She ordered the parties and their lawyers to attend a settlement conference before another judge in thirty days. If they were unable to reach a settlement they were to return to her courtroom in 60 days for trial.

While walking with Bleedem after the hearing, Mary was stunned to learn that the five-minute hearing at which nothing was accomplished had cost her $7,500 in fees.

Bleedem told Mary that he was going to need more money. She told him there was only $30,000 left. Bleedem asked if Joe had been helping himself to the cash? Mary said that he had taken some at the start, but then sent her a note saying that she could draw out of the bank accounts what she needed for fees and he would have to sell stock to pay his.

Bleedem immediately drafted and sent a settlement proposal Joe would certainly reject because, (1) It gave the house to Mary before dividing the other property equally; (2) it required Joe to give Mary 40% of his bonus

---

*Bubble & Squeak is an English dish made from the leftover vegetables from a roast dinner.

performance pay whether he earned it or not; (3) it required Joe to spend 500 hours a year on Gizmo for the next five years. Mary got 25% of any money Gizmo earned and Joe had to give her annual accountings of how he had spent that year's 500 hours. To frost the cake, he wanted Joe to pay $50,000 of his fees because it was Joe's attitude and behavior that had required him to spend so much time on the case.

The way it was written Joe couldn't accept the proposal without making an implicit admission that he had been reckless with his investment of community funds (even though there had been a market crash and even though he actually made more money than he had lost), and that he had attempted to steal the apartment building from Mary. To punish Joe, Mary would be getting the house before anything else was divided by two. This tacit admission of guilt for what he hadn't done ensured that Joe would never accept the proposal.

How Tactic VIII is done

At this point Bleedem was performing a final squeeze to obtain whatever fees he could get. Mary was paying attention so he had to do things that could be justified to her. He sent a settlement proposal designed and written so it could not be accepted, thus giving Bleedem a reason (excuse) to continue to work and to bill for that work.

Goode's analysis (below) was excellent. It explained how Bleedem would walk down a narrow path. On one side is the possibility of not billing Mary for work she should have paid for. On the other side was the possibility that he would do work and have a difficult time collecting payment for it.

The effect of Bleedem's tactic is described at the conclusion of the saga in the form of alternative endings.

The saga concludes

Bleedem's settlement proposal worked as he expected it would – maybe better. Goode was in an awkward position. He had a professional duty to communicate the proposal to his client, but he wanted to protect Joe from the admission of guilt. If he minimized those aspects of the proposal when he discussed it with Joe, he took the risk of being criticized for withholding information from his client. If he simply handed the letter to Joe or sent it to him in the mail, he ran the risk of having a client who was overwhelmed by the form of the message and who was unable to respond intelligently and deliberately to the content.

No matter how the proposal was delivered, Goode's unequivocal recommendation was against acceptance. He was on solid ground for two different reasons: (1) If the case were tried, it was extremely unlikely that Joe would come out as bad or worse than if he took the offer; (2) the terms of the proposal were so onerous that, if he accepted when it was offered, it would become completely unsatisfactory to him, days or weeks later when he regained his strength. If that were to happen, Joe's reconstruction of the past would pin the blame for the degrading settlement on Goode.

Goode arranged for Joe to come to his office. He gave Joe an outline of the proposal and then the letter itself. He let Joe express his feelings and offered to do the analysis at another time. Joe said that he was okay and asked Goode for his advice

Goode explained the range of their responses:

"There is no doubt in my mind that Bleedem wrote this proposal in a way that was so vile that acceptance would be impossible, which means that he didn't want to settle the case.

"I could be wrong, but I strongly doubt that he wants to try the case. This is an important premise so I want you to know why I think it's true:

(1) Fear. Very few divorce lawyers have accrued much in the way of actual trial experience, so he'll have some anxiety about having to actually try the case.

(2) The hit-and-run tactics he's used effectively during the last eighteen months don't work as well when the case has the judge's full attention for hours instead of minutes.

(3) The history of hit-and-run tactics may count against him in a trial. The judge noted the repeated references to the Hustler magazines, and I took that to mean that she realized Bleedem was trying to assassinate character as a way of bolstering arguments.

(4) Because of inexperience, he is likely to be clumsy in performing routine tasks and rituals during trial. He would prefer that his client not witness his weaknesses because that weakens his control over her and that jeopardizes his control over the flow of money for payment of fees.

(5) Once a trial starts, everyone loses control over cost and can even lose control over what direction the case takes. For example, the judge

could make a decision against Mary that, for any number of reasons, Bleedem would have to appeal. But Mary would be out of cash. Bleedem would file a motion seeking an order from the judge (the same judge whose ruling he is going to appeal) to sell stock to provide money for his fees to appeal her order.

"That motion might be denied, which would mean that Bleedem would have to do the appeal and wait to be paid at some uncertain time in the future. He wouldn't like that at all."

"If he does not want to settle right now and if he doesn't want to try the case, what's going on?"

"My guess is that he's going to take one last fee run at Mary. When he is coming to the end of the available cash, one of two things will happen. He'll somehow signal to Mary that she should talk settlement with you directly, knowing that you two will probably divide by two. Or, he'll call me for a 'lawyer to lawyer conversation.'

"My guess is that he'll approach a settlement in two phases. In the first phase his offer will be close; to make a rational decision to accept will require you to calculate the value of half the estate and subtract your anticipated trial costs. Let's say there was a joint estate worth $1 Million with potential trial costs to each side of $100,000. Bleedem would propose that you get $400,000, which is all you could expect if he tried the case and the court split the estate 50/50. He'd argue that it shouldn't make any difference to you if Mary gets more so long as you don't get less than you would with a trial.

"He'd probably find a way to say, 'Who do you want to get the money, Mary or your lawyer?'

"Of course, the same argument can be made in reverse, but we can be assured that Mary will never hear it from Bleedem.

"Anyway, I'd tell him his proposal is preposterous. I would communicate it to you, and if you accepted it, I'd call him back. If he didn't hear from me, he would assume that you saw his proposal for what it really was.

"He would then wait until the morning of trial. You and I would be all geared up to try the case, and he would have done whatever he could get paid for and nothing more. His last position – as he's planned from the start – would be a 50/50 split. He knows you'd have to accept it because you can't do any better.

"Judges are impatient when a trial turns to attorney's fees. If one side wins, shouldn't they also be awarded fees for the cost of the trial and then for the cost of proving the cost of the trial etc., etc.? Joe, this is a rhetorical question.

"We don't have to do anything until the settlement conference. After that, I can get this case ready for trial in thirty days. But there isn't a chance of settlement at that point unless Bleedem has come close to draining all the cash.

"If there is still some left, he'll do whatever he feels like doing to justify getting the rest of it. He can work to get those fees right up to the day of trial. He'll tell Mary that he is preparing for trial, and that's what the billing statements will show, but he'll never have to show in court what he did to prepare, because he can be sure of a settlement.

"If we were absolutely sure of this analysis, I would stop work on the case right now so you wouldn't have to pay me any more fees. But I can't be entirely sure. What if I've misjudged him, and he does prepare for trial? He still has a thin case, but that doesn't do you any good unless I can put on a case on your behalf. To do that I've got to prepare and that's going to cost money."

Joe asked, "What if I told you not to prepare?"

"Very good question. The answer is that I can't yield to a client who instructs me to be professionally negligent. I have a duty to you to refuse to follow that instruction. You might then say, 'Prepare as you will, but I'm not paying.'

"I would ask you to allow me to withdraw from the case. If you refused, I would petition the court for an order discharging me as your lawyer, but in making the request, I have to honor the attorney client privilege and can't explain how the circumstances compel my discharge. If the judge refuses to allow me to withdraw, I prepare to try the case in spite of your instructions. When the case is over, I sue you for those fees and you refuse to pay on the grounds that you told me not to do the work. And then a judge or jury decides that issue! Who pays the attorneys' fees in the litigation over attorneys' fees has to wait for another conversation."

Joe asked, "So where does that leave me?"

"With your approval, I will do what I think is minimum preparation to put on a decent but not the most compelling case possible. For example, if there were three witnesses who could each establish a certain fact, a well-prepared and presented case would probably call all three. Under these circumstances I'd call only one of them. Our trial brief won't argue the Joe whole case, but will be more like an outline. And we will be prepared to scramble.

"I'll get the firm to reserve time from associates and assistants so if the trial starts and we have to move quickly due to lack of preparation, we will. It's actually fun to do a trial that way, but you never know how it's going to turn out when you are shooting from the hip."

As the settlement conference approached Goode made a written proposal to divide the estate in two, including any income realized from Gizmo. Joe thought that he should get more that 50% of returns on Gizmo. Goode wanted to keep the offer as clean and as simple as possible, and Joe eventually agreed with him.

•••••

During the four weeks between the settlement conference and the trial, neither lawyer sent the other a copy of a complex trial brief. Neither called the other to address practical problems that come up in all litigation such as the organization of exhibits.

Bleedem billed Mary's case for lots of trial preparation. To show that he was working diligently he subpoenaed the principal of Joe's school, Frank (who was a witness to the discovery of the Hustler magazines) and the psychologist Joe finally went to see.

It took Bleedem seconds to sign those subpoenas – but once they were served by Jay Edgar, the responses would generate hours of conversation and consternation for Frank, the principal, and especially for Joe.

Endings

To describe the effect of Bleedem's endgame and Goode's response to it requires us to tell how the story ends. These are two possibilities:

Ending 1: The case goes to trial

For some reason, perhaps the ego of either or both lawyers, the case is actually tried before a judge. Bleedem is likely to have an unpleasant day or two in court, but when the trial is over, no matter how poorly he performed, he will send Mary a bill for every hour he spent in court and another hour during the same day for 'preparation' and a third hour for 'follow-up.' It is possible, even common, for a good lawyer trying a tricky lawsuit to spend eighteen hours a day working on a case that's actually in the courtroom for only six of them.

Strangely, the court cannot make rulings concerning the legitimacy of Bleedem's billings to Mary.

She can contest them in two ways: she can refuse to pay and Bleedem will have to sue her in an attempt to recover. Or, she can attempt to recover all or part of the money she has paid to him. She would do this by initiating a lawsuit or, in the alternative, by filing a complaint to the fee committee of either the state or local bar association. The complaint would be heard by a panel of lawyers. Some states add a non-lawyer to the panel. In most states, Mary can accept the decision of the panel and Bleedem would be bound by it, or she can reject it and go on with her lawsuit.

Ending 2: The paper napkin settlement

Bleedem was going to do what he could to dissuade Mary from 'interfering' with his management of her case and 'won't accept responsibility for the consequences if she does.' Mary didn't know what he was talking about, but it sounded grim.

As the time for the trial drew closer Mary felt increasingly anxious and frightened. Of all the people in the world it was Joe she would like to talk to. She had been with him for longer than she had lived with her parents, and even though they couldn't stay married, he still knew her better than anyone else. But Bleedem had convinced her that Joe was the enemy. If she didn't treat Joe like an enemy, she could, according to Bleedem, lose money in court. And yet, money had never been what was most important to her. The truth was that she wanted to talk to Joe, as her friend, about whether she could talk to Joe, the husband she was divorcing. She felt like she was Mary in Wonderland.

So Mary was grateful to get a phone message from Joe two days before the trial. She called him back and he invited her to go to dinner with him that night. He said, "I want to see if it might be possible finish this divorce on our own, and I think you'll be safe in a public place where I can't throw books."

"Joe, there's never been an opportunity to tell you that I have a much better aim than you do. Your book didn't come close to hitting me."

"I didn't throw it at you. It was still a dumb thing to do, but I threw it at the wall."

"What you don't know is that I did throw one at you just as you were leaving. If you hadn't slammed the door when you did, I think it would have hit you in the head. I think I talked myself into the belief that since it didn't hit you and you didn't even know it had been thrown, then I didn't do it. Like the tree falling in the forest with no one to hear."

"What went wrong with us?"

"I don't know, " said Mary, "but I've been thinking that I want to talk to you about this divorce and the trial as my friend, even if it turns out that it is too difficult to talk about getting this thing over with in spite of the court and in spite of our lawyers."

"I hadn't thought about it that way, Mary. I agree. I've kind of fallen apart since it's all began. I can't tell you the number of times I've thought that you were the one who could help me pull myself together, but I couldn't make contact with you."

Mary said, "The judge just gave us permission to talk to each other. How crazy is that? We've been married for fifteen years and we need a total stranger to decide if we can talk to us."

"I know, but she said we could, so let's do it."

Joe took Mary to a delicatessen, and she observed, "Our first dinner together for more than a year and you bring me to a place that has paper napkins."

He said, "Those lawyers have taken so much of our money that we may never again be able to go to a restaurant with cloth napkins."

"Since it's still joint property, maybe you could sell your photographic magazine collection and share the proceeds with me."

"Or, you can have the whole thing for nothing. You could give it to your lawyer, who seems to be fascinated by it."

"Joe, I understand why you didn't want anyone to know you had that stuff, and I had nothing to do with so many people finding out about it, but I've wondered why you had it, and realized that it might be because we stopped being intimate. Was that why?"

Joe said, "Duh."

With that out of the way they began work on their settlement. They agreed that their property should be divided equally, then Mary voiced her biggest fear, "Joe are you going to try to take the house from me or force me to sell it?"

"Mary, you love that house. If you still want it, I want you to have it."

"Of course I want it."

"Fine, it's yours. I'll take the apartments which are worth $70,000 less than the house, so I'll need something to make up the difference. But we have it and there will still be assets to divide between us."

"I thought the apartments were worth more than the house."

"They are, but we owe much more money on the apartments than we do on the house. When you figure out the value of a property to the person who owns it, you subtract what's owed against it from the fair market value. Generally, the value of property is what you could sell it for. That's what they mean by Fair Market Value. But when you figure out the value of a person's property, value is the money he would have after it was sold. So if you have a house with a fair market value of $500,000, how much would you expect it to sell for?"

Mary answered without feeling as though Joe was lecturing her, "I guess $500,000."

"Yea. The fair market value is always an estimate, but for the example let's say it sold for $500,000. But the owner had a loan against it of $100,000, which gets paid off out of the proceeds from the sale. So after the loan is paid, what's left for the seller?"

"I get it, $400,000."

"Right, and if that owner, before the sale, determined what the property was worth to him, what would it be?"

"Still $400,000."

They put the apartment and the house in brackets with the difference in values being something they would go back to.

Next, they agreed that they didn't have to worry about dividing their cash and some of the stock they had at separation because it now belonged to the lawyers. Mary asked, "Do we have enough money for me to have dessert?"

"Have five if you want."

Next Joe explained that when they divided the remaining stock, they had to be careful to divide it in such a way that they took into account the basis – the purchase price – because the bigger the difference in value between the original cost and the ultimate sale, the greater the capital gains tax.

Mary asked, "Are you saying that if you got one of our Apples and I got another and we both sold ours for, say, $300, that one of those shares was worth more that the other? That doesn't make sense."

"You are probably missing two pieces of the puzzle. The first is capital gains tax. When you sell a share of stock for more than you paid, you have to pay tax on that profit. The second missing piece is that you have to keep track of the price you paid for every share of stock you own and of what you get when you sell it."

"So how does that work with the two Apples?"

"We each get one Apple and we each sell the one we got for $300. However, the share you got was purchased for $150 and the share I got was purchased for $250. Who got the better deal?"

"What difference does it make if we each got $300?"

"If we bought your Apple for $150, what's the profit if we sell for $300?"

"$150."

"When the Apple purchased for $250 is sold for $300, what's the profit?"

"$50."

"Okay, to make it simple, let's say the capital gains tax is 10% of the profit."

"How much tax would you pay on your profit of $150 and how much would I pay on my profit of $50?"

"You would pay $5 and I would pay $15. But that's only $10. Who cares?"

"Well, we still have about $160,000 in the stock market so it could add up. It's easy when we can each get the same stock with the same basis. But I still need $70,000 to balance the difference in the values of the house and the apartments. If we turn that problem over to the lawyers, we will have a lot less stock to worry about dividing. This is a problem they'd love to get their teeth into."

"Joe, I'm not sure that I understand it. Are you saying that you can divide it up instead of the lawyers? I think that would be okay with me."

"No, I could do it but I want to have it done by someone else. I suggest just about anyone other than the lawyers. If your father would do it that would be fine. I don't know the stockbroker very well but I think he would do it if we both asked, or we could asked the accountant who does our taxes. We don't know her very well, and she'd probably charge a fee, but so long as she doesn't get paid to fight with another accountant, it shouldn't cost very much. Or, you could find someone else."

"You decide."

"Our accountant."

"You will follow up on that?"

"Sure."

The conversation went on in a similar way. Neither drank alcohol. Neither felt emotional. They didn't bargain and they didn't negotiate. They didn't say things like, "I'll do this if you do that." Instead, it was a conversation between two intelligent, well-meaning people who had a problem to solve.

It was a problem to solve, not a war to win, not a game to win, and not even a deal to negotiate.

Next, they talked about spousal support. They both understood the law to say that because they had been married for a long time, the court would keep the case open so at any time in the future one could ask the court to order the other to pay spousal support. They also understood that this was a right they could give up.

At this point Joe confessed that he was afraid of losing his job. Mary had heard rumors about Joe's trouble at school. She felt she might be responsible for some of his problems, but she didn't feel guilty enough to want to support him. It was she who suggested that they really get the case over with and give up the right to go to court *for anything* in the future.

"If we each give up the right to go back to court that would keep it simple, and Joe, you keep Gizmo. I hope you get something for him."

Joe replied, "If I lose my job I would have plenty of time to work on him, and really Mary, he might turn out to be something good. The offer made by Bleedem said that any profit from Gizmo would be divided 50-50. I didn't like it. Let's say I spend a year working on Gizmo and someone buys him. If we split that profit 50-50, you would get half of Gizmo plus your teaching salary for the year, which would be more than I would get for creating him."

Mary said, "I agree. That wouldn't be right. But what if you got nothing for him, would I have to give you half of my salary?"

"Oh, no," said Joe. "I'll take the risk of failure. And it might take me two or three years or longer to get him working."

Mary said, "You should be well paid if you work on Gizmo and you sell it. I don't want to invest by supporting you while you work on him, so you
    should get even more than fair pay because the risk is all yours. But, Joe, it started while we were married. If you sold him at $100 million or even $1 million I would feel like a fool and that I betrayed myself if I got nothing."

Joe said, "If Gizmo sells for a Million or more, I get the first Million, and we split everything exceeding $1 Million, 25% to you, 75% to me."

Mary said, "How about 35% after the first $500,000?"

They went back and forth in this fashion and finally decided to flip a coin – twice. The first flip would decide whether Joe would receive the first $500,000 or the first $1Million before he had to share with Mary. Joe won. The second flip was to decide whether Mary would get 25% of the profits after the first $1M or 35%. Mary won that flip.
    Then they decided to make the threshold $750,000 before the split and if they made the split, Mary would get 30% after the first $750,000 and Joe would get the rest.
    What they finally decided could be written down on one side of a folded paper napkin. They agreed that they would ask Goode to write the formal agreement and to take care of whatever had to be done with the court.
    Before they left the restaurant they made sure that their napkins contained exactly the same summaries of the deal.

The Paper Napkin Settlement

House to M for 380

Apt to J   for   310

J to get 1ˢᵗ 70 from stock   70

Lawyers got cash   0   0

Stock 160-70 = 90   45   45

(broker to divide =ly]

each keep own pension

no spousal support

If something else to be decided J & M to work it out: no lawyers

---

House to M for 380

Apt to J   310

J to get 70 from stock   70

Lawyers took cash

Stock 160-70/2   45   45

[broker to deal with basis & divide =/y]

no spousal support – each keep own pension

Gizmo = 1ˢᵗ 750 to J and thereafter 30% to M.--No lawyers if problem M& J to work out

ENDNOTE #1 – The Settlement Proposal

Bleedem's Settlement Proposal begins on the next page, 76.
Each section is followed by analysis and commentary in the gray shaded boxes.

Bleedem & Bleedem
Attorneys at Law
Practice Limited to Matrimonial Litigation
123 Courthouse Plaza
Orlando, Mind 11111
888-233-3333

Mr. Allen B. Goode
Fair, Goode & Goode
25 Huntington Plaza, Third Floor
Orlando, Mind 11111

RE: Marriage of Martin Comprehensive Settlement Proposal

Dear Mr. Goode:

Since the court has set a settlement conference for four weeks hence, I am getting a jump on the process by making this settlement proposal at the first opportunity so that you and your client will have all the available time to consider its terms. If accepted, we would not have to appear at the court supervised settlement conference.

One of the few things legal ethics require of a divorce lawyer is to communicate with the client the terms of a settlement proposal from the other side. It is uncertain whether a summary or the actual document containing the proposal has to be passed on to the client. On the one hand, the lawyer may want to shield the client from unduly upsetting language. On the other hand, a summary of several interrelated provisions may fail to pass on subtleties that won't be captured in a summary. It is Goode's policy to always give the letter to the client, with a detailed commentary if he thinks it necessary. In the alternative he will ask the client to come to his office to first read and then react to the letter in his presence. This is quicker, but it also entails the possibility that the client may psychologically mistake the messenger (his own lawyer) for the originator (Bleedem).

There is nothing untoward in this first paragraph of Bleedem's letter until it is understood in the context of the entire letter. It creates the impression that the settlement is one that is worthy of "all the available time to consider its terms," when it is clearly unworthy of serious consideration. It is also vaguely patronizing in that it states the obvious: that acceptance of its terms would obviously avoid contact with the court and both Joe and Goode are fully aware of that fact.

By the time of the settlement conference, my trial preparation will have already begun, and it will be in full swing immediately after an unsuccessful conference. At that

time, I will clear the decks of my own practice and devote
myself to trial prep on a nearly full-time basis.

*Goode knows this statement is hogwash and included as Bleedem's attempt to
intimidate Joe just as he did with the Slimeball at the outset of the case. This time
Joe has been through the meat grinder and is hardened to this kind of attack, and
he has Goode to act as both a filter and a buffer. Nevertheless, the statement that
someone will "clear the decks" to put his operation to prepare a case against you
into "full swing" and "on nearly a fulltime basis" is disconcerting – few of us have
ever had anyone say such things to us. The inclusion of the word "nearly" is another
touch of professional bullying. Saying "nearly fulltime" instead of "fulltime" conveys
verisimilitude because the claim is moderated by the adverb "nearly," which
conveys an apparent desire for accuracy.*

This letter is a proposal of settlement and compromise and
is therefore privileged under Evidence Code Section 1234.
Moreover, Rule of Professional Conduct 5321 requires you to
communicate this settlement proposal to your client.

*It is customary to make it clear that the letter is being sent as a privileged document
(cannot be used in court as evidence). But it is insolent for Bleedem, of all people, to
remind Goode of his ethical duties.*

1.Division of Property

    a. Ms. Martin to receive the house off-the-top, and
       she will assume full responsibility for paying the
       entire balance of the unpaid note.
    b. The apartment building to be sold and the proceeds
       divided equally.
    c. The cash and securities to be divided equally.

*There's the essential case in six typewritten lines. The problem is that it should be a
single line that says:*

"Divide our property equally." That is definitely not what Bleedem's letter says.

*Chapter 8 Endnote 1 explains with numbers why a division that starts with
distribution "off the top" and concluding with "divide the rest equally" is not an
equal division.*

*The last thirteen words in paragraph **1. Section (a)**. contain a subtlety that will require three paragraphs to explain. These words won't mislead Joe, but they could confuse a person unfamiliar with basic financial ideas and the language used to express them. The subject of the sentence is Mary; she is "to receive the house" (four words), which is something she acquires. Mary also "assumes the full responsibility for paying the entire balance of the unpaid note," which reduces the value of the house. Notice how it takes Bleedem four words to describe what Mary gets and thirteen words to explain how the value of the house is reduced by assumption of the note.*

The proposal distributes the house to Mary without a corresponding distribution to Joe. The more the inequality can be minimized, the less its negative impact. Even Bleedem can't disguise the fact that his client gets a house and her husband doesn't, but by using four words to describe what she's getting and thirteen words to describe what she's giving up, Joe's first reaction might be "no" instead of "hell no."

Instead of using thirteen words, Bleedem could have communicated the same substance by saying, "Ms. Martin will receive the house-off-the top, and she'll assume the note."

[Note: With the economic circumstances existing since 2008, it is common for a person to receive a house or other building or even a car and to assume responsibility for the debt associated with it and end up with property that has negative value. This happens when the size of the debt secured by the property is bigger than what that property could be sold for. This is what is meant when a property is described as "upside-down."]

To summarize: Giving Mary the house, with Joe getting nothing in exchange, makes this proposal a non-starter and Bleedem knows it.

2.The Gizmo

This presents a difficult problem. I have only one solution to offer, and it is admittedly awkward. If you have other ideas, they will be welcomed and considered. If the Gizmo is ever marketed, or if the rights to the Gizmo are transferred, Ms. Martin will receive 1/4 of the proceeds. The notion here is that half of the Gizmo was created during marriage and the second half will be created after marriage. My client will get one half of the money realized by a completed product. Your client will warrant that he will spend no less than 500 hours per year on the project for the next five years. This approximates the amount of time he spent in his shop during the marriage. We realize that he might have been doing something else during his time behind the locked door, but this is our best estimate. Mr. Martin will be required to keep time records of his activities on the Gizmo and deliver a copy thereof to me between January 2 and January 31 for the next five years. In order to enforce the intent of the agreement either party may, by noticed motion, request the court to fashion a remedy to that end.

We think most of our readers will not go past the second line of this complex and convoluted proposal. It makes Joe a slave to this project. A working year is usually considered to be about 2,000 hours long. Bleedem wants Joe to promise to work on Gizmo for 500 hours a year for five years. In other words Joe must work on the project for an equivalent of 2500 hours or 1.25 years, whether he's getting anywhere with it or not. And he must provide Bleedem(!)with proof that he did the work.

This scheme is so unworkable that the size of Mary's share doesn't make any difference. But when quantified, the proposal is shown to be even more dubious. The arithmetic isn't simple, but for Mary to be entitled to 25% of the profits after Joe spent 1.25 years on the project after marriage, he would have had to have spent an unlikely 6,250 hours on Gizmo during marriage.

3.Spousal support

Your client is paid more money than mine — even though they are both teachers with the same number of years in service to their respective school districts. Whatever Mr. Martin has that makes him more valuable to his district than Ms. Martin is to hers was developed during marriage, so it is therefore fair and legally necessary that Ms. Martin share in his good fortune. We propose that for spousal support Mr. Martin will pay to Ms. Martin an amount equal to 40% of the difference between his gross pay and hers. The payments may be made on a monthly or annual basis. Ms. Martin will pay tax on these payments if, and only if, Mr. Martin is entitled to the corresponding deduction.

The justification for this demand is not illogical, but how much difference could there be in the pay for two teachers in geographically proximate districts who both started to teach at the same time? If Joe truly gets substantially more money than Mary, it's likely to be because he works longer hours. If this is the case, he shouldn't be required to share with her the benefit he gets from the extraordinary hours he spends working.

In some states, under certain conditions spousal support is determined by reference to a schedule. The schedule is based on a formula. A typical formula would award no support if the "low earner's" income is equal to 80% or more of the "high earner's income." So there would be no support ordered if she earns $100,000 per year and he earns $80,000, or if he earns $50,000 and she earns $40,000.

Neither my client nor I is interested in annual struggles to determine how much more Mr. Martin earned than Ms. Martin (or how much Ms. Martin would have earned should she leave her teaching job for any reason). We also know that Mr. Martin is able to win annual bonuses awarded on the basis of his students' success because he has done so for the past ten years. Therefore, if he should fail to receive a bonus in the future, it is fair to assume the failure was due to some volitional act on his part, and Ms. Martin should not suffer for that. Therefore, we are willing to set the difference between his and her school compensation at $_____, of which 40% or $_____ would be paid to` Ms. Martin. These payments, regardless of Mr. Martin's employment or lack thereof, shall continue until Mr. Martin reaches the age of 65, until one party dies or until Ms. Martin remarries, whichever occurs first.

This is crazy! First it assumes that Joe will continue to win an annual bonus for the rest of his career, when, in fact, his termination is being considered because of the discovery and great to-do over the Hustler magazines. To add insult to injury, Bleedem says that if Joe doesn't get the bonus it's because he blew it with an intentional act. Furthermore, he has to pay Mary 40% of the difference between what he earned and what she earned at the time of divorce — even if he is unemployed.

4.Attorneys' fees

Mr. Martin's behavior and attitude toward the legal work that had to be done to properly represent Ms. Martin has doubled the fees that would otherwise have been generated. By the time the case is wrapped up, we guess that Ms. Martin's total fees will be in the neighborhood of $120,000. Therefore, as a part of this settlement, Mr. Martin should pay this office $60,000, which will pay any remaining balance on Ms. Martin's account, with the rest going to her.

Getting one spouse to pay another's attorneys' fees is always difficult. It is usually better to side-step the fee argument with a concession on some other point. The best way to preclude discussion of whether one party will pay some of the other's fees is to work out a generous concession on a different point that more or less substitutes for a fee award.

Note that Bleedem has to justify his claim against Joe by saying that his "behavior and attitude toward the legal work that had to be done...doubled the cost."

Even if Joe were willing to pay some of Mary's fees (an unlikely event because of who represents her), he would never do it if it came with this tacit admission that it was he, not Bleedem, who caused the legal expenses to be so inordinate.

5.Waivers, etc.

Any right to compensation for the rental value for the use of a joint asset, e.g., Mr. Martin's use of the apartment building unit, will be waived. Any right to reimbursement for expenditures during separation shall be waived.

This is fine so far as it goes, but, to keep the record clear, it should say that Joe is waiving the right to claim the fair rental value for Mary's use of his half of the house. Bleedem would argue, "Of course Mary doesn't pay rent on Joe's half of the house because he has lost any interest in the house because of the various ways he violated his fiduciary duty to Mary." Since the violation of his fiduciary duty has been trumped up by Bleedem to generate fees, this is another way to tie Joe's thinking into a knot with more circular reasoning.

Although the investigation being carried out on behalf of Mary Martin to determine what, if any, joint assets were converted to Joseph Martin's use by whatever means was not completed, in part because of Joseph Martin's intrusion, Mary Martin will also waive any claim she may have against Joseph Martin originating with the collection and maintenance of pornographic materials, without her knowledge, at the home they shared after marriage and prior to separation.

When a divorce is settled, the parties want it settled completely. If Joe were to accept the agreement as Bleedem summarizes it here, Joe would have to make a tacit admission that he did what Bleedem recklessly accused him of doing solely for the purpose of generating fees for himself.

I trust that you and your client will give this proposal the attention it deserves and respond to me at your earliest convenience.

     Sincerely,

          George P. Bleedem

               George P. Bleedem, Principal
               Bleedem & Bleedem & Associates
                    Attorneys at Law

ENDNOTE #2 – "Off-the-Top"

Bleedem put together a settlement proposal he knew would not be accepted. This created the superficial appearance of a willingness to settle. He had two reasons for this. The first move is called "anchoring," a term used to explain that "research shows" that a negotiator who begins with a very low offer does better than one who begins with a 'reasonable offer.' The second reason, it should come as no surprise, was to generate fees.

The analysis shows how some provisions favor Mary in ways that are not entirely transparent. The one most disadvantageous to Joe is the distribution of the house to Mary "off the top." Mary has never claimed that Joe deceived her and, according to the facts in the story, he did no such thing. What the story shows is that Bleedem was able to find "evidence consistent with fraud," which justified more discovery – and the greater the discovery the bigger his fees. "Evidence of fraud" is not the same as proof of fraud. In the proposal, Bleedem attempts to use evidence as though it was proof.

Joe knew Mary wanted the house and he wanted her to have it, but he thought he would get something of equal value in exchange. The devil is in the term "off the top." This means that the home equity goes to Mary before the division of the other assets. It will look like this:

	Value	Mary	Joe
Equity in house	$380,000	$380,000	
↑ THE TOP ↑			
Equity in apartment	$310,000	$155,000	$155,000
Cash at separation [before lawyers]	$126,000	$63,000	$63,000
Stock [before lawyers]	$190,000	$95,000	$95,000
Total	$1,006,000	$693,000	$313,000

Thus the award of the house equity to Mary "off the top" gave her $380,000 [$693,000 – 313,000] more than half and $380,000 more than Joe.

To equalize, Joe gets ½ the difference. Add $190,000 from his share and subtract that amount from Mary's.

ENDNOTE #3 – Divide by 2

"It isn't true that divorce lawyers can't divide by two. They all can do it. The problem is that they come up with different answers."

A FOOLPROOF WAY TO DIVIDE BY TWO

Step one: Determine the "net value" (also called the "equity") of each joint asset. If an asset is associated with a debt, subtract the debt and deal with the remaining "net." If you own a house with a value of $600,000 with a mortgage (or a note secured by a trust deed) of $200,000, the net value (and the equity) is $400,000.

Step two: Add up the values of all the joint property equities. Subtract the amount of the debt not associated with (not secured by) any one asset, for example credit card debt.

Step three: Divide by two. This number is half the value of the net joint estate. The ultimate test for the division of joint property is whether each spouse gets the Step 3 amount.

Different Ways to Divide the Same Pie

Wife and Husband own:		
	Home equity	$400,000
	Rental Property Equity	300,000
	Savings	200,000
	Stock	100,000
	Credit card debt	-80,000
	Net total	920,000

Each party should get the value of $920,000/2 = $460,000.

1. To Husband: Home, ½ savings, ½ stock, and ½ debt = $400+100-40 = $460,000. No more counting required.

2. To Wife: Rental, savings, entire debt and $40,000 of stock. $300+200+40-80 = $460,000. No more counting required because if Wife gets half, what's left is half.

3. To Wife: House, stock, and ½ debt = 400+100-40 = $460,000.

Appendices I - IX

Appendix I

Joe, Mary & Money

Joe and Mary had no children. They had been frugal and managed to accumulate $150,000 in savings and $150,000 in a brokerage account. They owned a home and a six-unit apartment, where Joe eventually went to live.

Mary had no interest in money. Her paycheck went into a joint checking account which always had a balance high enough for her to buy whatever suited her modest lifestyle.

Joe was not much more interested in finances than Mary. He had his check deposited into the joint account, and as their cash began to accumulate, Joe felt that they should "get their money to do at least a little work for them." On various occasions he tried to discuss finances with Mary, and she always changed the subject. He understood her silence and attitude of indifference as permission for him to do his best to handle their finances in whatever way he thought best for both of them.

Over the years Joe bought and sold stock and averaged five trades per year. After seven years of marriage, he purchased a small apartment house from a friend. Six years later he traded up for a property that was bigger and delivered a higher return on the investment.

Joe told Mary about the apartments; she wasn't interested. The brokerage account statements came to the family home and were addressed to "Joe and Mary Martin." Joe made regular transfers from the joint checking account to the joint savings account. He had a second "investment" checking account, which was set up in his name alone because he didn't want to bother Mary by asking her to go to the bank to sign a signature card for a joint account. He never deceived Mary about their finances; he never intended to take advantage of her and he never intended to hide any information from her.

Overall Joe did better in the stock market than a fund indexed to the Dow Jones. In other words he "beat the Dow Jones," which is considered to be the hallmark of competent money management. But he didn't beat the Dow Jones by much.

He would insist the Enron fiasco taught him that if an investor could not rely on the veracity of a company's financial statement, how could anyone but an insider make knowledgeable trades? Nevertheless, he kept joint funds in the market and made trades on what he perceived as the quality of the company and its products.

When his investment history is studied, it is clear that he has had only one stock that increased in value and outpaced the Dow Jones, and that was Apple. Without the (unrealized) gain in Apple, Joe's investments would not have increased as much as the Dow Jones. In fact, he lost money on most of his trades.

He's done better with real estate. The down payment for the first property was $30,000. Ten years later the value of the equity in the second property is $300,000.

Appendix II

Even More About George Bleedem

George is fifty-two. He is married and has three children. The nature of his personal life affects the way he practices law. He lives in a contentious atmosphere very similar to the one he grew up in. His children have an attitude of scarcity; they believe that both within and outside the family there will never be enough of anything for anyone. This includes tangible possessions, attention, and approval. George and his wife have the same attitude.

George, his wife, and their children spend a lot of time with George's brothers, sisters and their spouses and children. They all see the world in black and white and believe there is an external, objective reality that some people understand and some don't. They continually disagree and argue about the nature of this objective reality, but they believe that, while they may have their differences, the Bleedem Family "gets it" as well as any other family and a lot better than most.

It is this fundamental belief system that makes George and his family so disagreeable. While they can argue indefinitely about who is right, they believe there are only two ways to prove it: make money and prevail over other people. To prevail over others at every opportunity and to make money are the reasons George is an attorney.

George's father was a criminal defense lawyer who didn't give George much in the way of paternal approval. If alive, George's father would look down on George as a divorce lawyer, even though George makes a point of earning more income in every year than his father did in any year.

George wasn't good at school sports and frequently found a reason for being excused from changing for P.E. He's not good at other kinds of games, so he avoids them. He has learned to be a fierce and feared competitor as a divorce lawyer. He puts a lot of energy into his cases, and he is sincerely determined to "win," which means prevailing over the other lawyer and party. Ultimately, however, being well and fully paid takes priority over "winning the divorce."

Because his client and the client's spouse are at one of the most vulnerable times in their lives, he can always prevail over both of them.

George has been exposed to the idea that divorce shouldn't be adversarial, and that it is about division by two. It is what his father thought. But George has convinced himself that only cowards, losers and peaceniks would espouse such a view. He treats each case as a contest between him, the other lawyer and the other spouse. Because it can be so profitable, George likes to "fight for the woman."

Since he sees each case as a fight, he always gets one. On rare occasions he has contemplated how he benefits from a fight and how little work he would have if the parties were encouraged to reach their own settlement. This thought comes to him when, after representing a client for a year or two, he is told that she and her husband have met and have worked out a settlement that can be summarized on the back of a paper napkin. When she says that she wants no more fighting and only a settlement agreement, George is grateful that he generated his work early and was paid for it before the parties came to terms with each other.

When business is slow, George will instigate activity in one or more of his pending cases. Whatever he does can be justified both ethically and against any challenge to his billing. Yet he realizes that he doesn't stir the pot in a case when he has other work to do.

When a case gets particularly hot and heavy, George has a connection with two legal assistants who work from home and by the hour. When George has something for them to do, he bills their time at $150 per hour. He pays them $50, and George keeps $100. [In a law firm, a case requiring the services of legal assistants is welcomed. The owners of the firm (the partners) get to keep the difference between the fees the assistants generate and their share of overhead and what they are paid. Typically this works out to $\frac{1}{3}$ compensation, $\frac{1}{3}$ overhead, $\frac{1}{3}$ profit; thus, a good associate or assistant becomes a "profit center."]

George sees all human interaction as competitive, and he deals with many people who, under most circumstances, would be more competent, smarter, and more personable than he. During a divorce, these same people are extraordinarily vulnerable. George's drive to dominate, the vulnerability of the parties, and the absence of effective ethical constraints on the exercise of his power as a divorce lawyer combine to create an unfortunate psychological dynamic that leads to George's subjective belief that as a Kick-Ass-Litigator he serves Mary by taking her money to dominate and to wound Joe.

To those not blinkered by familiarity with the typical Rules of Professional Conduct that protect this kind of practice, George is a bully who takes advantage of the temporary weakness for his own financial gain and as an opportunity to wound people over whom he has circumstantial power. With this behavior he experiences compensation for all the times he has been dominated by others.

Appendix III

About Allen Goode

Allen Goode is a junior partner in the 30-lawyer firm of Fair, Goode & Goode. He is not a name partner; the Goode in the firm's name was Allen's grandfather, who has been dead for a decade. Allen is a lawyer because everyone in his family is or was a lawyer and because there was always a job at his grandfather's firm waiting for him.

The firm specializes in construction law, which Allen dislikes because it doesn't involve people. While he's not delighted to be practicing family law, it is all about people. The main reason Allen hasn't been made a partner is money; he doesn't bring in enough and the partners are always either prodding him on or scolding him for a poor performance.

Allen's billing is low because he bills only for work he actually does, and he always resolves any billing questions that occur to him in favor of the client. He doesn't like the way family law has cloaked its work to look like real civil litigation with ongoing motions to the court and "formal discovery." Allen doesn't see the necessity of complicating what's simply a listing of assets and an accumulation of facts that create the context for a division by two. Allen has found that when he leaves a divorcing couple alone for whatever time it takes, they come to terms with each other. Less "lawyering" seems to be better than lots of "lawyering," but it makes it more difficult to earn a living.

From what he has observed in his practice, he suspects that almost all divorcing parties can resolve their issues in their own (best) way – if they are encouraged and allowed the necessary time and space. That being said, he welcomes a good fight because it is with hotly contested cases that he can earn enough money to keep the partners off his back. He has also come to believe that if the lawyer on the other side of a divorce case is determined to "stir the pot," there is nothing Allen can do about it other than to defend his client as though his client was being prosecuted by the District Attorney's Office.

And that's something he knows how to do. He worked as a deputy in his county's district attorney's office for seven years before he joined his grandfather's firm. He has learned how to try cases to juries and, compared to that, any divorce case is a walk in the park. If he and George Bleedem's father were to have a conversation about George, they would agree that whatever George is doing is not about practicing law. [If George were to hear of such a conversation, he would counter by saying that he always makes more money than Allen, and that he has made more money in every year of his practice than his father made in any year of practice. George's father would reply, "But look what you are doing to get it."]

Both by disposition, family history and values – and by his training and experience as a prosecutor – Allen is a decent man who actively seeks ways to ensure that what he does in his work is consistent not only with his personal sense of ethical imperatives, but also with the prescribed Rules of Professional Conduct. When he was a prosecutor and encountered defense lawyers who had given up their personal values and sense of honor in order to better serve their criminal clients, Allen felt pity for what the lawyer had become and disgust for what they did.

As a prosecutor Allen could afford this kind of attitude because of the enormous advantage he had from the start. Judges and juries do not want criminals to go free. When he encounters the same thing in a divorce case, he rarely knows what to do. He won't sacrifice his own sense of honor to enter into an illusory battle with someone who has spent years thinking about the best ways to skirt the Rules of Professional Conduct, how best to take the cheap shot, and how to get into the parties' bank accounts.

Appendix IV

Mary Lawyers-up

Joe and Mary are two decent people who have come to a "parting of the ways." As the song says, "There are no good guys; there are no bad guys." If left to their own devices, they would be able to work out a way to divide their property in two. Nearly all couples need time while they grieve the loss of the partnership, so immediate settlements are not the rule.

Here, Joe didn't want the divorce and will need time to adjust to his new reality. The same is true for Mary, even though she is the "Initiator." It will also take her time to gear up and take responsibility for her own finances.

When Joe entered the house with his key, Mary was surprised, angry and frightened. For one thing, she wondered what would have happened if she had been entertaining a male friend when her husband decided to stop by uninvited. Forget about men, what about her? She put a lot of energy into renovating the apartment so it would be a very good place to live. Joe, who wouldn't move out of the house, instantly takes the apartment when he's given his choice, but now, apparently, he thinks he has the run of the house too. Mary has felt very emotional, especially since the separation. She's not afraid to feel and express those emotions – but not with Joe.

When Joe wouldn't give into her demand for the key after their heated argument, she felt powerless and incapable. This made her feel frightened, and frightened people get angry.

She hired George Bleedem on the recommendation of a friend who "heard" from a friend of a friend of a friend that Bleedem was good at representing women who were not financially sophisticated. Mary made an appointment to see him the next Monday afternoon.

Bleedem talked more than he listened, and he told her that he would require a retainer of $20,000 – to be followed by additional retainers of $20,000 whenever her account balance dropped to zero or below. She was somewhat surprised by the amount, but she figured he must be worth it or he wouldn't ask for so much. Besides, she knew she had the money.

Back to Bleedem and how he sees his task

George Bleedem has been doing this work in the usual way for so long that there is at least a chance he doesn't fully appreciate that his economic interests and Mary's financial interests are far more opposed than the financial interests of Mary and her husband. The more work George does, the more he makes on the case.

George has learned that if he always assumes the worst about the Other spouse and practices on that assumption, the Other will usually rise to the bait and perform as Bleedem predicted. Whether this happens or not, Bleedem can always claim that his aggressive style is the best overall way to provide his client with the "zealous" representation prescribed by the American Bar Association or the "vigorous" or the "assertive" representation prescribed by rules of professional conduct in many of the fifty states.

In this case a settlement would be a matter of dividing by two, and attorney involvement could be limited to preparing the technical documentation necessary to put into effect the agreement reached by the parties. That is not a practical way for a divorce lawyer to approach a case because he wouldn't be able to make a living. The time required to document most settlements is so minimal, and the resulting fee so low, that most divorce lawyers don't want to handle a case that requires no other "services."

Bleedem wouldn't want the Martin case if he didn't see how it could yield enough work to be "worthy of his talent." To him, the positive qualities of the Martin case are: (1) There are substantial assets; (2) There is enough cash to pay substantial fees on both sides; (3) His client is naïve and dependent; she won't think of trying to control or limit what he does; (4) She is attractive and pleasant, which makes her easier to deal with over time; (5) Joe is a high school teacher. He won't know what hit him. He is likely to anger, and when angry he is likely to act with his emotions and against his own best interests; (6) Because of the availability of cash, whoever Joe hires will not be afraid of a "good fight;" (7) It is not a case where anyone is going to really win or lose, it's a matter of who gives up. In any event, the likelihood of a trial, which is very stressful for the lawyers, is extremely remote (<4%) and, in a pinch, the case can always be settled by dividing by two!

As attorney for the Petitioner (the Petitioner is the initiator and the Respondent is the other spouse), Bleedem has a one-time opportunity to make direct contact with the Respondent. This is done with a letter delivered with the Petition and Summons. The most invasive and aggressive way to deliver these documents is to use the services of the Sheriff's Office, which has a duty to provide for the "service of process" in all matters originating with the court.

The most civil way to deliver the documents is by sending the package by mail; that's what Bleedem does. The letter he sends urges Joe to get his own attorney immediately, which seems responsible of him. But this letter is a "Slimeball." Its implicit message is:

'*Mary has hired a battalion of lawyers and legal assistants who are going to investigate, at Joe's expense, every aspect of Joe's handling of the marital estate and, no matter what they find, they will use it to prove that Joe did something wrong.*'

Appendix V

Joe's despair after the hearing

Home to lick his wounds, Joe decided that the toll taken on him since the conclusion of the first "nightmare hearing" was unbelievable. The "Incident of the Hustler Magazines" was, up to that time, the most humiliating experience of his life.

He had never before been humiliated so deeply and in so many ways. When Mary returned to her home the magazines were opened to create a display worthy of a porn shop, even though Joe had never set foot inside of one. The same couldn't be said of the ubiquitous Jay Edgar who took so much delight in his find and in following Bleedem's directions in a way that would exploit the situation to maximize Joe's embarrassment.

For Bleedem, Joe's immediate mortification was but the beginning. In documents that would become part of the public record of the divorce, Bleedem alleged and argued wherever he could that Joe's possession of the materials constituted a "violation of his fiduciary duty to Mary in his management of community property." Because the "community received no benefit" from Joe's purchases, Joe had, in effect, stolen Mary's half of the community funds used for their acquisition.

The total amount of Joe's expenditure was less than $200 and was therefore insignificant relative to the couple's annual income of more than $100,000 and even more insignificant relative to the marital estate of more than $1,000,000, but Bleedem contended that it could be the tip of the iceberg and as Mary's attorney his duty to provide "zealous" representation required him to investigate that possibility. In determining the scope of his responsibility, Bleedem didn't compare the cost of his "investigation" to the probable benefit to Mary. How could he? The service to Mary was not to find evidence of Joe's misappropriation of assets but to extinguish Joe's ability to continue with the "litigation" and force him to settle the case on whatever terms, however unfair, Bleedem dictated.

Joe's reluctance to rent a truck to move his property from the house resulted in the ill-fated presence of Frank Meredith. As soon as he arrived at work the following morning, Meredith told every teacher he saw about the incident. By the end of the week word had spread throughout the school district, whose administration was always on the alert for teacher behavior that might be a signal that the moral development of students could be in danger.

In spite or because of the Hustler incident, Joe worked hard on the proper completion of the Comprehensive Disclosure Statement, even though he would have preferred to be doing anything else. He thought he had completed the complicated and time-consuming task on time, only to discover that he'd have to pay his lawyer to defend him against the charge that he had failed to provide Mary's lawyer with documents located in the house where Mary was living and the house from which Mary's lawyer had had him excluded.

Joe understood why his lawyer, Allen Goode, thought they should attempt to show the judge how Joe was being bullied by Bleedem. He approved the expense but, when he read the final version of the brief, he realized how likely it was for the judge to fail to understand what Goode attempted to explain about the dynamics of bullying. After all, a third of all teachers believed that bullying was a part of the normal adolescent experience schools could ignore in all but the worst cases.

To say the judge didn't understand what Goode wrote about bullying was an extreme understatement. Joe was ordered to pay Mary's lawyer $1,000 as a fee for reading what his own lawyer had written – at a cost to Joe of $12,000. The total cost to Joe for the principled and utterly unsuccessful fight against the bully was $13,000. What Joe did get for his $13,000 was an order that allowed him to go to his own house, now in Mary's exclusive possession, to search for documents that had been demanded by Mary's lawyer. No matter how many documents were found and turned over to Bleedem, Joe was confident that Bleedem would claim the production was inadequate and the inadequacy was proof of a criminal act or, at the very least, Joe's criminal intent.

Even though Joe was quickly losing confidence in his own lawyer, he noticed that he was becoming less intimidated by unexpected contact with Jay Edgar; it wasn't of much comfort but it was at least something.

Appendix VI
[Tactic V]

The *Ex Parte* Garbage Can Hearing
&
How George Bleedem "Hit From Behind"

Chapter 5 starts with the story of how Bleedem assigned Jay Edgar to stake-out Joe's garbage can the night before Joe was required to turn-over any other Hustler magazines or any other writing that included photographs of women without clothing. Bleedem's theory was that instead of turning over more embarrassing magazines, he would keep them until the last minute and finally dump them into his garbage. Indeed, Edgar observed Joe deposit two shopping bags into his garbage. Edgar seized the can, wrapped and sealed it in plastic and substituted a new can of the same size and quality.

The next morning Bleedem made an ex parte request to the court to schedule a hearing as soon as possible. Absent a good reason, a court should not disrupt its procedure for handling business in an orderly and predictable way. According to Bleedem, the need for an emergency hearing was he wanted to break the seal on the garbage can so that its contents could be inspected in open court under judicial supervision.

To keep the main text concise, the story jumps from the time Goode gets notice of the hearing at 8:05 a.m. and the court's ruling at noon. This appendix contains the following:

- The boxing metaphor for Chapter 5 is "Hit from behind." This refers to the "kidney punch" and the "rabbit punch" prohibited in nearly all kinds of pugilistic sports. We explain how each is delivered and why they are both prohibited.

- Punches that hit from behind are similar to two kinds of applications for an ex parte hearing. We explain what an ex parte hearing is and why it is like being punched from behind.

- A description of Allen Goode's reaction to the notice of the ex parte hearing is followed with the transcript of what Bleedem said in court and how Allen Goode responded. The story then continues in the main text with the transcript of the judge's ruling, which was both unexpected and refreshing.

Two kinds of hits from behind

A kidney punch is opportunistic and delivered when one fighter has been maneuvered so, for a second or two, his back is turned to his opponent who has sufficient room to cock his favored arm and deliver a very hard blow to either side of the lower back where a kidney is located. The punch is illegal because it comes from behind so its victim doesn't see it coming and therefore can't defend against it. As a target, the kidneys are not protected by a bone structure and therefore particularly vulnerable to injury. One hard punch to a kidney can render the recipient incapable of continuing the fight.

A punch directed to the junction of the cervical spine and the brain stem is called a "rabbit punch" because it mimics the way hunters dispatch rabbits they've shot but not killed. The punch is thrown when the recipient cannot see it coming and cannot defend against it. A vicious rabbit punch can permanently injure or even kill its victim.

Two kinds of *EX PARTE* hearings

CONTEXT AND VOCABULARY

The correct translation of *EX PARTE* is "of or from one side (only)," which, in the language of the law, is a judicial decision made after a HEARING on evidence and argument presented by one side only. A hearing is a mini-trial of a subject incidental to the main issue in the case. A hearing is initiated with a written MOTION, which describes an ORDER the judge is being asked to make and the EVIDENCE that supports the request. The first function of the MEMORANDUM OF POINTS AND AUTHORITIES is to identify the law giving the judge authority to make the order when adequate EVIDENCE has been presented. EVIDENCE is either witness testimony or a tangible object such as a document. The second function of the MEMORANDUM OF POINTS AND AUTHORITIES is to describe how the evidence presented and the applicable law combine to warrant the RELIEF (synonym for Order) requested. A LAW AND MOTION CALENDAR carries more than one case – sometimes dozens – to be disposed of within the time the judge is allotted for entire calendar, typically two or three hours. Evidence is commonly presented in DECLARATIONS, which are narratives written on paper with numbers running down the left margin and signed under penalty of perjury.

When one party wants to SET (schedule) a hearing on a motion, the NOTICE OF MOTION designates a time and date when the court hears its law and motion calendar. That date must be far enough in the future to give the other party the time allowed for a RESPONSE and for the initiating party to have time to file a REPLY to the RESPONSE. Normally, the period between the delivery of the NOTICE OF MOTION and the date of the hearing will be about three weeks.

In contrast, an *EX PARTE* hearing will be held within forty-eight hours of the court's receipt of the APPLICATION.

When the notice of a hearing is less than forty-eight hours (four hours in this case), work on anything else must be dropped and existing appointments, no matter how important, must be cancelled or postponed. Lawyers don't keep track of a client's daily activities, but when a hearing is scheduled on short notice, the client must be located, informed of what has happened, and told when to be at the courthouse. Often, the RESPONSE should include a DECLARATION by the client, which means obtaining his side of the story, reducing it to written form and acquiring his signature in time to get the document filed with the court before the hearing. The party who sets a hearing on short notice will often be able to prepare the MOVING PAPERS at leisure, while the other party and his lawyer must stop whatever they are doing and refocus their attention on the imminent hearing, even if the matter at issue is of minimal significance.

In family law there are no jury trials, so a TRIAL means a proceeding before a judge where there is time for the live testimony and cross-examination of witnesses and both opening and closing arguments from the attorneys. When a trial date is set the parties and their lawyers will have 60 to 90 days to subpoena witnesses and to prepare a TRIAL BRIEF, which is more detailed but functionally the same as the MEMORANDUM OF POINTS AND AUTHORITIES used for hearings.

The practice of making judicial decisions after an *EX PARTE* hearing runs counter to a core principle of Anglo-American legal philosophy (JURISPRUDENCE), which is the belief that "truth" is best discovered when the two opposing parties enter into a DIALECTIC, which is a discourse in which the side seeking the court's action must produce evidence meeting a specific standard of proof and survive the cross-examination and testimony from additional witnesses produced by the other party. Since American judges are not allowed to actively investigate the cases they hear, a decision made on evidence offered by one side only has not been subjected to a truth filter (cross-examination and testimony by other witnesses), and it won't include the other side of the story.

In general, and for good reason, American judges dislike EX PARTE proceedings and discourage their use.

1. *EX PARTE* HEARING (ONLY ONE SIDE PRESENT) ON A REQUEST FOR SPECIFIC ORDER

Sometimes, however, a court must make an *EX PARTE* order because the potential harm that could result if relief is delayed for the usual notice period is significantly greater than the harm caused if the order is granted with what could turn out to be insufficient justification. This is especially true of the first kind of *EX PARTE* application where one person tells the court that an order must be made to prevent the occurrence of something bad, wrong and irrevocable.

A common example is the temporary restraining order issued to prevent the continuation of domestic violence. The alleged victim describes a history of violence and threat of future violence and asks for an order instructing law enforcement agencies to keep the alleged perpetrator away from the alleged victim, which will require the exclusion of the alleged perpetrator from his own house. If, after a full adversarial hearing it turns out that the alleged perpetrator is innocent and has been wrongfully excluded from his house for a few days or weeks, that harm is much less serious than the probable injury to the alleged victim if what she said had been true and it took the court weeks to provide her with a protective order.

2. *EX PARTE* APPLICATION FOR IMMEDIATE ADVERSARIAL HEARING (ONLY)

The second kind of *EX PARTE* application doesn't ask the judge to make a one-sided decision about an issue in the case. It seeks only to have the court schedule a hearing on very short notice. The other lawyer is always surprised when told to prepare for and appear at a hearing to be held in a matter of hours. She must stop what she's doing, clear her calendar until the hearing has been completed, locate and contact her client, and prepare a written defense.

The first type of *EX PARTE* hearing is held to consider a substantive request. ("Keep him away from me and out of our house." Or, "prevent him from taking our child out of the United States.") The second kind of EX PARTE application asks "only" for a radically expedited adversarial hearing where both sides will be presented. And yet, the *EX PARTE* application that seeks only an immediate hearing is the one most easily abused.

As you read the description of Bleedem's case and how he makes it, ask yourself what he's really trying to accomplish. There is no single correct answer; our answer is printed at the end of this Appendix.

•••••

Allen Goode drafted a declaration in which Joe denies that there were Hustler magazines in the garbage can, and then he started a Memorandum of Points and Authorities to raise a legal objection to the seizure of the can. Goode then had to write a legal argument against the request to open the can and study its contents. He started with an empty mind and blank computer screen. Because of his experience in criminal law, Goode was familiar with the huge body of law that prescribes what does or doesn't constitute a legal search and when evidence that's discovered as the result of an illegal search must be suppressed.

He started to look up a number of appellate court decisions to refresh his recollection about their details but soon realized that his knowledge of criminal law was taking him to a dead-end. The suppression of illegally-seized evidence is a policy directed toward law enforcement agents who know that if they make illegal searches, whatever they find cannot be used in court. Neither Jay Edgar nor George Bleedem was a law enforcement agent, so suppression of evidence would not serve the social policies that regulate the conduct of the police.

Goode couldn't develop a decent argument when he analyzed the case from Joe's perspective or from the perspective of society as a whole. He let his mind drift and thought of a third point-of-view – the other occupants of the apartment.

He assumed everyone living in the building had a reasonable expectation that what they put into the garbage would not be examined by a third party who was investigating the personal life of one of the occupants of the building. Then assume that while the reason for suspecting that Joe would attempt to destroy evidence was very thin, it was specific enough to override *Joe's expectation of privacy*. But what about the other occupants? Their only connection with Joe and Mary was the payment of rent. Why should the fact that their landlords were a divorcing couple compromise the tenants' expectation of privacy by allowing a disbarred lawyer to seize garbage and to then pick through it in open court?

Once he could articulate a legal reason for keeping the can sealed, Goode decided not to ask Joe to sign a declaration. Goode was worried that Joe might give a false declaration that said there were no Hustler magazines in the can when, if fact, there were. He might do this to avoid immediate embarrassment and in the hope the contents of the can would not be inspected. If the defense failed and the can was opened and Hustler magazines were found in the garbage, Joe's perjury would be immediately apparent and his honesty on all issues would be compromised. Trading credibility for futile attempt to avoid embarrassment is a bad trade-off, so Goode decided not to take the risk.

•••••

Because it was he who was asking the court to make an order, Bleedem was the first to speak.

"Your Honor, we have in court a garbage can sealed in a plastic bag. We are here on my application for an ex parte order for an immediate hearing. The garbage can was seized and sealed last night by my investigator because I determined there was probable cause to believe that it contained evidence relevant to issues in Marriage of Martin.

"The nature of the evidence is thought to be a heretofore undisclosed part of Mr. Martin's pornography library or collection – whichever he chooses to call it – and evidence of his schemes and designs to convert joint property to his own use.

"The evidence begins with the fact that today is the last day for Mr. Martin to comply with my demand for production of documents. The demand specifically asks for pornographic material other than the sizable collection hidden in his shop at the house he once shared with my client, Ms. Martin.

"I also demanded any documents evidencing Mr. Martin's plan, scheme or design to deprive Ms. Martin of her interest in joint property. The basis for this demand was our eventual discovery of the fact that Mr. Martin has managed to acquire and hold what should be the couple's most valuable asset, a six-unit apartment in his name and in his name alone.

"Mr. Martin delivered to my office his first version of a Comprehensive Financial Statement. It was incomplete. One of the things missing was the deed to the apartment building. Mr. Martin claimed that he didn't attach a copy of the deed to the Comprehensive Financial Statement because the deed was located in the house from which he had been excluded.

"I thought this was strange at the time because he could have obtained a copy of the deed from the County Recorder's Office or from any title company in town. But he didn't. He tried to argue that Ms. Martin actually had possession of the deed because she was living in a house where the deed was 'stored somewhere.' His plan is obvious. He hoped that we would accept his argument and conclude the case without following up on the acquisition of the deed.

"Furthermore, your honor, for the past several years Mr. Martin kept all records relating to jointly-owned property in his so-called 'shop' where the pornography library was discovered. Who knows what he did in his "shop," but it had a locked door so that he could keep Ms. Martin away from the pornographic material and away from the records of whatever he was doing in his attempt to convert their property to his property.

"Because he was under the pressure of the deadline, it was my belief that he would hold on to his smut until the last possible moment and then attempt to dispose of it rather than complying with my discovery demands. From the time Mr. Martin came home from work yesterday afternoon, my investigator was positioned so he could see the garbage cans used by the residents of the apartment. At 8:17 PM my investigator observed Mr. Martin, whom he has encountered on three previous occasions, deposit two shopping bags full of *something* into the can that was seized and delivered to this courtroom.

"On my instructions, my investigator conducted reconnaissance of the service area of this apartment. He made note of the size and brand of garbage cans available for use in the service area. With this information, he went to Home Depot and purchased a replacement can of the same size and brand, which made it possible for him to sequester a can, as he has done, and to replace it with a can of equal size and quality."

The judge didn't look thrilled with Bleedem's presentation, but she had let him talk without interrupting him, which meant that she was probably listening. When called on, Goode did something very difficult for a lawyer to do. He was brief.

He wanted to remind the judge that he was appearing after notice so short that he and his client had not been able to meet. The inspection of garbage was not sufficiently urgent to warrant a hearing that disrupted his and his client's ordinary business days. He wanted to ask the court to fine Bleedem for abuse of the judicial process by seeking an emergency hearing on a trivial issue. However, the judge had already permitted the hearing to be scheduled on short notice, so she had already decided the *ex parte* application for the immediate hearing was appropriate. It's usually futile to attempt to change a judge's mind once she has made a decision and acted on it.

Goode said only:

"So under the circumstances, I will say nothing other than to point out the obvious, and I will do it with concision. The garbage cans served all the tenants of the apartment. So if there is a right to not have investigators pawing through your garbage, it's their right too. If they have a right to be free of invasive excursion into their waste, there must be a legal justification for violating that right. What does Mr. Bleedem have to justify the invasion of the tenants' privacy? That's all for me."

The kind of judicial relief sought by such an *ex parte* application is often less important than the meta-message sent to the other side when a hearing is set with very short notice. Here, the real communication to Joe is:

When *you* least expect it and whenever *I* feel like it, I can Hit You From Behind by getting a judge to order you and your lawyer to drop whatever you are doing to prepare your response and then haul your butts into court to answer the allegations I'm making against you. I don't care whether I win or lose as long as I demoralize. I hope you will ask your lawyer, "Why don't you do the same thing to him and Mary?" He will say, "What would be the point other than to run up fees for her and for you too?" Then you will say, "I want her to know how this feels." Your lawyer will reply, "Fighting fire with fire accomplishes nothing except to make a bigger fire." Then, maybe you'll insist that he "stand up" for you by being more aggressive – more like me. Oh please, insist that your lawyer be more aggressive; make my day.

Return to the main text, page 45, for an account of the court's refreshing ruling.

Appendix VII

How lawyers and law firms make money – a short course

Like anyone who works by the hour, self-employed lawyers (those who work by themselves or those who are one of several partners who share the profits from a firm and are not paid a salary) get to keep what they earn less the cost of earning it. Overhead can differ widely. Bleedem keeps his overhead to a minimum, so he gets to keep most of what he is paid.

Goode is a "senior associate," which is a nice way of saying that he's been a paid employee for several years. Typically, associates stay with a firm until a decision is made to accept or to reject them as partners. Six years is a common period between initial hire and "the partnership decision." Associates who are passed over for partnership leave the firm and are replaced by law school recruits.

A lawyer's own effort produces his earnings, but it's the work of associates and legal assistants that generate profit. The formula is simple. Divide an associate's or assistant's income by three. One third should be enough to pay salary; another third should be enough to pay for the overhead associated with the employee; the last third goes to the firm. Law firms talk in terms of the partner to associate/assistant ratio. The higher the number of associates/assistants (or the lower the number of partners), the more money the partners make. For example,

Assume billings = collections	Overhead	Employee Compensation	Profit
Associate = $225,000 $225,000/$200 p/h =1125 hrs 1500 hours x $200 = 300,000 1800 hours x $200 = 360,000	$ 75,000 100,000 120,000	$ 75,000 100,000 120,000	$ 75,000 100,000 120,000
Assistant $150,000/ $100/p/h = 1500 hours	50,000	50,000	50,000
Profit generated by one associate and one assistant. If there is only one partner for every associate and one for every assistant, each partner earns an extra $150,000.			$150,000

The challenge to running a law firm on this model is having enough work for the associates and assistants on the payroll. In the example we assumed that the associate was billing $200/hour. To simplify, we also assumed that the firm was able to collect everything it billed (which would be unusual). In the first example, where the associate has only 1,125 hours for the year, they are either unemployed or lazy. The standard measure of a fully employed lawyer is 1,500 hours per year. A large firm with highly paid associates will expect them to bill 1,800 hours (a killer schedule). Some will bill 2,000 hours per year (and will probably die young).

The second challenge to running a firm on this model is hiring and retaining associates and assistants who are capable of doing the work.

A solo practitioner like Bleedem who has work-from-home assistants will be able to keep 66% of what he bills their time for because he pays them, but he doesn't have to provide an office, secretary, etc.

Goode is a senior associate, which means that he gets a salary. It also means that his firm is expecting him to bring in some of his own business so a portion of his 1,500 to 1,800 hours a year will be attributable to clients who come to him rather than clients who come to the firm and are assigned to him. According to the facts in our story, Goode is having difficulty bringing in enough work to stay busy and to generate income.

With a case like this Goode has to do the work even though he thinks it is a farce. By doing the work he increases his hours, which increases his income to the firm, which enhances his chances for being made a partner.

In other words, Bleedem is making money on this case in the form of his own earnings and profit from his work-from-home legal assistant. Goode is on salary and gets nothing extra for working on the case. However, if the income to the firm from this case helps Goode get a partnership instead of a dismissal, it could be worth more to him – over his years as a partner – than what Bleedem is squeezing out of Mary.

Assuming Goode is good at heart, could his determination to limit the amount of unnecessary time on a case like this be compromised by his long-term economic interests?

Appendix VIII

Combined Billing Statement

Appendix for Chapter VI: Attorneys' Fees to Date.

The table on the following pages shows the legal activities in the left column with estimates of the maximum number of hours Bleedem and Goode could probably get past a Bar Association Fee Arbitration panel. We assume a billing rate of $300 per hour, which is low for work in a medium size city (> 50,000 population) and probably high for smaller cities.

Description of Services Part 1	Bleedem Professional Services Attorney @ $300 p/h (per hour)	Bleedem Professional Services Legal Assistant @ $150 p/h	Goode Professional Services Attorney @ $300 p/h	Goode Professional Services Legal Assistant @ $150 p/h
Initial conference w/ client: draft Petition, Summons & design case management plan	6.5	2.5	4.0	2.0
Draft initial letter to opposite party	2.0	0	0	0
Prepare notice of motion and supporting documentation for Temporary Restraining Order (TRO) re return of key, exclusion from house & attorney fees	6.0	6.0	0	0
Prepare Opposition to TRO			4.0	2.0
Reply to response to Motion for TRO	4.0	4.0	0	0
Review Reply	0	0	1.0	1.0
Prepare for, attend, & follow-up on Superior Court hearing	6.0	4.0	6.0	4.0

Description of Services Part 2	Bleedem Professional Services Attorney @ $300 p/h (per hour)	Bleedem Professional Services Legal Assistant @ $150 p/h	Goode Professional Services Attorney @ $300 p/h	Goode Professional Services Legal Asst. @ $150 p/h
Draft letter re completion of Comprehensive Financial Statement	2.5	0	0	0
Receive letter re completion | analyze | discuss with client			2.0	0.5
Review & Analyze Comprehensive Financial Statement	6.0	2.0	4.0	2.0
Prepare Notice of Motion documentation re completion of Comprehensive Financial Statement	6.0	2.0	0	0
Prepare Opposition to motion | investigate circumstance | confer with client	0	0	6.0	2.0
Prepare for court, appear in court on motion, Follow-up	6.0	2.0	6.0	2.0
Prepare comprehensive set of Interrogatories, coordinated with document production & deposition	8.0	12.0	0	0
Receive & review interrogatories, analyze, discuss & deliver to client review answers provided	0	0	8.0	12.0
Receive, review, summarize & analyze answers to interrogatories	10.0	20.0	0	0

Description of Services Part 3	Bleedem Professional Services Attorney @ $300 p/h (per hour)	Bleedem Professional Services Legal Assistant @ $150 p/h	Goode Professional Services Attorney @ $300 p/h	Goode Professional Services Legal Assistant @ $150 p/h
Prepare notice of motion to compel answers to interrogatories, appear	6.0	12.0	0	0
Receive motion to compel, prepare Response	0	0	4.0	4.0
Prepare motion re protective order and "bully memo"	0	0	40.0	40.0
Receive and review notice of motion re protective order (extensive supporting documentation)	8.0	4.0	0	0
Prepare Reply to Response to motion to compel further answers to interrogatories	5.0	2.0	0	0
Prepare Response to motion for protective order	16.0	12.0	0	0
Receive and analyze Response and Reply	0	0	6.0	4.0
Prepare Demand for Documents (105 items)	6.0	12.0	0	0
Prepare for, attend & follow-up on court hearing	6.0	6.0	6.0	6.0
Review and Analyze documents produced	12.0	24.0	0	0
Prepare notice of motion re production of documents and supporting documents	6.0	12.0	0	0
Receive & analyze document demand	0	0	4.0	4.0

Description of Services Part 4	Bleedem Professional Services Attorney @ $300 p/h (per hour)	Bleedem Professional Services Legal Assistant @ $150 p/h	Goode Professional Services Attorney @ $300 p/h	Goode Professional Services Legal Assistant @ $150 p/h
Organize and arrange surveillance on garbage can	4.0	6.0	0	0
Prepare pleadings for conduct of judicially supervised search of garbage can	8.0	3.0	0	0
Prepare Reply to Response to motion for production of documents	6.0	2.0	0	0
Prepare for Court Hearing re production of documents, protective order & supervised search of garbage can	6.0	6.0	6.0	6.0
Prepare settlement proposal	3.0	0	0	0
Receive, review & analyze settlement statement	0	0	2.0	0
Conference with client re settlement	0	0	2.0	0
Prepare subpoena (x 3) & arrange for service	1.5	4.0	0	0
Preparation of Trial Brief (Bleedem)	16.0	4.0	0	0
Research re applicable law	8.0	5.0	0	0
Prepare for Direct Examination of Witnesses	5.0	3.0	0	0
Prepare for Cross Exam of Respondent's Witnesses	4.0	3.0	0	0
Final settlement discussion	2.0	0	2.0	0

Description of Services Part 5	Bleedem Professional Services Attorney @ $300 p/h (per hour)	Bleedem Professional Services Legal Assistant @ $150 p/h	Goode Professional Services Attorney @ $300 p/h	Goode Professional Services Legal Assistant @ $150 p/h
Prepare Marital Settlement Agreement	0	2.0	3.0	2.0
Discuss & correct MSA	2.0	0	2.0	0
Prepare court documents	0	0	2.0	3.0
Review court documents	2.0	2.0	0	0
Total Hours - Attorney	168.5 hours		120 hours	
times $300 p/h	$50,550		$36,000	
Total Hours – Legal Assistant		162 hours		96.5 hours
times $150 p/h		$24,300		$14,475
	24,300		14,475	
Total Bleedem: $50,550 + $24,300	$74,850			
Total Goode: $36,000 + $14,475			$50,475	
Total fees =	$74,850 +	$50,475	=	$125,325

Appendix IX

The deposition from "day-to-day" until completed

"Abandon hope all ye who enter here."

It started off with a lot of righteous pontificating by Bleedem. To Goode it was the same old "bla, bla;" to Joe it was incomprehensible jabber, but when he was asked if he understood, he said that he did because he wanted to get it over with. This was even though he had been told by Goode, at least three times, maybe more, that any attempt he made to truncate the deposition would have the opposite effect and it would be prolonged.

To the usual final admonition, Bleedem added a flourish: "Mr. Martin, we may come to the point where I ask a question and Mr. Goode tells you not to answer it. I can either let it go or I can ask our judge to compel you to provide the answer. If this happens, I will ask the court reporter to cite you into court on May 25th at noon, which is a date and time she was given by the court clerk. So, if you refuse to answer a question, we will suspend the deposition for as long as it takes for the court reporter to cite you into court. Then, we will proceed with the deposition on issues that are not closely related to your refusal to talk.

"If we have a court hearing, the judge can make any order she wants to about attorneys' fees, but it's my experience that judges tend to award fees to whomever wins on the most issues. If Mary has prevailed on any issue, we will leave court, return to this room, and complete your deposition. Do you understand?"

Joe said that he did and was determined to answer any question he was asked. The interrogation began with the list of fifteen years of stock transactions. Bleedem asked a series of very detailed questions about every trade. In fifteen years there had been, according to Joe, a total of 123 buy or sell orders, or about eight per year.

Bleedem then asked about the first purchase of stock. "Where did you get the money to buy it? How much did you pay? How many shares? Why did you buy this stock?"

Joe started to say "I don't recall," but Bleedem had a sheet of paper describing the stock's 'fundamentals' at the time of purchase. He asked Joe if any of the ratios were familiar to him. Bleedem then asked if Joe knew anything about investing in the stock market. Joe said that he did but had trouble explaining just what it was. Goode threw a life preserver and objected to the question on the grounds that it was too vague. He forced Bleedem to continually narrow the inquiry until it was simple enough to be answered with a couple of sentences. Undaunted, Bleedem asked the same questions and Goode made the same objections.

Bleedem asked the same dozen questions to which there had not been an objection with respect to every transaction.

As a physicist Joe was pretty good at numbers, but he also talked too much when given a chance to explain something he knew about. But he still didn't remember why he bought this particular stock fifteen years before. When Joe finished, Bleedem asked fifteen more questions about the second transaction, and Joe had to say, "I don't know."

Bleedem jumped from the earliest transaction to the most recent, asking the same fifteen questions and getting essentially the same answers. Then he went back to the second transaction, asked the same questions and got very similar answers. By the time it was noon, they had gone through four trades. If he were to ask about the next eight transactions during the afternoon, they would have covered only twelve out of 123 trades; this could be a ten-day deposition on the management of the stock alone.

Joe did some reckoning: if the depositions took 6 hours per day at $300 per hour, the attorneys' fees for each side would be $1,800 per day. The fees for a ten-day deposition would be $1,800 times ten days for a total $18,000 – minimum – for him and also for Mary. It would be a $36,000 deposition.

Goode was so bored that on the fourth day he was in a near-trance when Bleedem slipped in the question, "What did you do with your pornographic library behind the locked door of your so-called shop?" Before Goode could speak, Joe countered, "When?"

Bleedem nearly rubbed his hands together, "Well, let's see. Maybe you should tell me. What were the various activities involving the use of your pornographic library, and then you can tell me when you participated in each."

Goode interrupted, "Objection, irrelevant; Joe, don't answer."

Bleedem said, "It is a proper question because it is reasonably calculated to lead to discoverable material. I'm seeking evidence on the issue of whether Mr. Martin's pornography collection was of any benefit to Ms. Martin."

Goode shot back, "No. We have not made any claim of that nature. I don't think you are seeking admissible or discoverable material. You are trying to humiliate my client again. You've had your fun and now you need to stop. We stipulate that these legal magazines published for men did not benefit Ms. Martin at all and, at the time of the division of property, Ms. Martin should receive an amount equal to the total cost of the magazines with ten percent simple interest from the date of publication. In fact, to eliminate this ridiculous issue, we are prepared to stipulate that the total value of the magazines Mr. Edgar discovered was $500, which is a number I've selected because it must be worth several times the market value, if there is a market value for this stuff. And Mr. Martin agreed to give half of the magazines to Mr. Edgar and the other half to you. If there ever was a legitimate reason for these questions, it just disappeared."

Bleedem, glad to get a rise out of Goode, said smugly, "I'm under no legal obligation to accept your stipulation, and I don't. Does Mr. Martin still refuse to answer the question?" Goode said that he did and Bleedem told the court reporter to cite Joe into court, and the court reporter did.

Bleedem immediately asked a similar question from what looked like a list. It got the same reaction from Goode, Bleedem had a similar response, and the court reporter cited Joe again and again and again until Bleedem had asked questions with ten variations on the same theme, and Joe had collected ten citations, which sounded pretty bad. In spite of Goode's reassurance, Joe couldn't help but wonder and fear that when you are "cited" ten times, there has to be a good chance you could go to jail. Even though he couldn't think of what he did wrong, Joe was feeling increasingly guilty.

A half day was spent on the fact that the deed to the apartment was in Joe's name alone and another half-day was spent on the location of the financial records in the shop. Joe's answers were all the same, "Mary wasn't interested in finances. She thought it was a man's job to do. I did it even though I was almost as disinterested and bored with it as Mary was. We were alike in at least that one way."

Who knows what inspired Bleedem to ask Joe about the energy company, Enron, but it resulted in answers to questions he would never have been asked if he hadn't been happy to talk about something he had studied and a subject on which he had an opinion.

The gist of this line of questioning boiled down to Joe's statement that Enron proved that investing in the stock market was irrational, prompting Bleedem's follow-up question, "So why did you leave Mary's money in the stock market after you had this realization?"
Where can Joe go from there?

Q   Back to the stock trades: "Mr. Martin, in mid-2000 Enron's stock reached its all-time high of about $90 per share. It fell to less than a dollar a share in November 2001. Are you familiar with the basic outline of the story?"

A   "Yes."

Q   "Did you see the movie, "The Smartest Guys in the Room?"

A   "Yes."

Q   "Did you follow the story in the newspapers?"

A   "Yes."

Q   "In national magazines?"

A   "Yes."

Q   "Did you follow the trial of Jeff Skilling?"

A   "Yes."

Q   "Did you have conversations with friends and with colleagues at work about the story?"

A   "Yes."

Q   "How many?"

A   "Dozens."

Q   "Did you ever buy Enron stock?"

A   "No."

Q   "Did you form any opinions about the case or about the stock market in general?"

A   "Yes."

Q   "What was one opinion you formed about the case?"

A   "That the higher management, especially Lay and Skilling, were as corrupt as I think a human being can become. They were absolutely despicable."

Q   "Do you think they were more despicable than I am?"

A   "No. They were just smarter and working on a much bigger stage, a bigger scale."

Bleedem seemed pleased by the reaction he got.

Q   "Thank you at least for making that distinction. What opinions did you form about the stock market?"

A   "It confirmed for me something I had long suspected. If the financial statements prepared by Arthur Andersen were not only inaccurate, but also fraudulent – and Fortune still named Enron its most innovative of admired companies in 2000 – then I don't think it's possible to make rational decisions about the value of any stock."

Q   "So the whole thing is corrupt?"

A   "Look at what's happened since: it's not a "market" where everyone has access to the same information – it's a market where a few know what's going on and the rest are dupes who may or may not come out okay. It's luck."

Q   "When did you reach this conclusion?"

A   "When with respect to what? Are you asking for a specific date? For an 'ah ha' moment?"

Q   "An approximate date would be fine, or it could be relative to some development in the story or in one of the lawsuits or criminal prosecutions."

A   "Sometime in 2002. I learned that immediately after Skilling dumped a half-million shares, Lay was telling employee shareholders that everything was rosy."

Q   "You do know a lot about the story."

A   "It was formative."

Q   "What do you mean by that?"

A   "I said it when you started with these questions. Enron confirmed my worst suspicions about the stock market."

Q   "I want the record to be perfectly clear on this. You concluded that the stock market was corrupt and that investors could not make informed and rational decisions about what to buy and when to buy it before the end of 2002. Is that correct?"

A   "Yes."

Q   "Mr. Martin, if you decided that the stock market was corrupt and rational decisions could not be made by the end of 2002, why did you continue to buy, sell and hold stock right up to this day in 2011?"

A   "Mr. Bleedem, that may be your first good question in this case. I wish Mary had asked it or had been willing to listen to me when I talked about the whole thing."

Q   "What 'whole thing?'"

A   "Investment."

Q   "I didn't ask you about what Mary would or wouldn't do. I asked why you stayed in the market."

A   "Some combination of greed and fear – and a touch of pack mentality."

Q   "Can you explain?"

A   "I'll try. After we had been married for about five years, it was clear that we could live in a way that was comfortable for both of us on just a little more than one salary, even after we bought the house. Our savings built up quickly, and we were paying lots in taxes. My strategy was to try to make enough money in a rising stock market to offset, at least in part, the income taxes we were paying. I kept what we had in the market to about a third of our savings."

Q   "Did it work?"

A   "Sometimes it looked like it did. We'd be up from our original investment and then we'd be down."

Q   "Did you think you were wisely investing in the stocks you bought?"

A   "Never."

Q   "What do you mean?"

A   "I always thought it was just chance."

Q   "So why did you, or why do you, do it?"

A   "As I said before, it's a combination of greed and fear."

Q   "You say neither you nor Mary was interested in money and yet you tell me now that you invested in a market you thought was corrupt because of your greed?"

A   "I think so. It's a kind of greed that has to do with the fear of being left behind if you don't take a risk. With the ever-rising market and low interest rates, I guess I was concerned about being the only people in the country afraid to go for a ride on the big boom."

Q   "Why did you think you would be the only people not to ride?"

A   "That's hyperbole. But it seemed like what I've read about the 1920's. I heard lots of people talking about their investments and their gains, and they weren't what I would think of as investor types."

Q   "Such as?"

A   "My barber! The people behind the counter at the deli, and teachers in the faculty room. The stock market was the number one topic of conversation until the crash. Then it became a taboo subject."

Q   "Did you take advice from your fellow teachers?"

A   "No, never. *That* would be reckless."

Q   "How so?"

A   "The ones that have advice to give are instant experts. The math teacher thinks he understands the market because he was a math major and can do algebra faster than the kids in his class. Of course he's been solving the same equations for years. Anyway, he's a self-proclaimed expert and talks of the market as if it were human. The market has likes and dislikes; sometimes it gets depressed, and so on."

Q   "I still don't understand why you invested in something you don't believe in."

A   "I think to be part of it. To be in on good fortune and not left out. That's all, and that's why I didn't go over a third of what we had. Even if we had lost every penny, it wouldn't have changed the way we lived. So the greed was wanting more than we had, which was already more than enough."

Q   "Did you discuss any of this with Mary?"

A   "No. She did not want to talk about money. Period. It got to the point where it would have been disrespectful to bring up the subject when I had been asked repeatedly, and then flat-out told, not to do it."

GOODE INTERJECTS

"Counsel, you know, of course, that the investments Mr. Martin made over the course of the marriage show a gain. You can ask question after question about what he did or didn't do, but even if he made investment decisions by throwing darts (and you could prove that that was a bad way to make decisions), the fact remains that there was no damage."

Q   "Mr. Martin, is the unrealized gain on your shares in Apple that make it possible for you to say that, overall, you have a portfolio that's worth more than what you put into it?"

GOODE

"Objection, irrelevant for the reasons just given."

Q   "Are you instructing him not to answer?"

GOODE

> "No. I'm trying to help you see that what you are doing is a waste
> of time and money."

Q   "Lucky for me this is my deposition, and I'm the one who decides
what is and isn't worthwhile. It's your interruptions that are a waste
of time and money, so when you feel the need to speak, why don't
you write a note to yourself and save your client the expense of
having us all listen to whatever it is you are compelled to say."

> "Now, Mr. Martin, about the several purchases you have made of
> Apple stock…"

And so it went for five full days.* The questioning on the stock market
went somewhat faster than Joe feared, and he also answered questions
about how he supposedly tried to steal the apartment building from Mary
and how he supposedly kept her from having access to their financial
records.

*As of January 13, 2013, California depositions are limited to seven hours,
unless the limit is extended by court order.

www.ingramcontent.com/pod-product-compliance
Lightning Source LLC
Chambersburg PA
CBHW050509210326
41521CB00011B/2391